CAUCASUS REGION POLITICAL, ECONOMIC AND SECURITY ISSUES

ECONOMIC REFORMS IN POST-COMMUNIST GEORGIA

TWENTY YEARS AFTER

CAUCASUS REGION POLITICAL, ECONOMIC AND SECURITY ISSUES

Additional books in this series can be found on Nova's website under the Series tab.

Additional e-books in this series can be found on Nova's website under the E-book tab.

CAUCASUS REGION POLITICAL, ECONOMIC AND SECURITY ISSUES

ECONOMIC REFORMS IN POST-COMMUNIST GEORGIA

TWENTY YEARS AFTER

VLADIMER PAPAVA

Nova Science Publishers, Inc.
New York

For permission to use material from this book please contact us:
Telephone 631-231-7269; Fax 631-231-8175
Web Site: http://www.novapublishers.com

NOTICE TO THE READER

Library of Congress Cataloging-in-Publication Data

Economic reforms in post-communist Georgia : twenty years after / editor, Vladimer Papava.
p. cm.
Includes bibliographical references and index.
ISBN 978-1-61942-542-2 (hbk.)
1. Georgia (Republic)--Economic policy. 2. Georgia (Republic)--Economic conditions. 3. Post-communism--Economic aspects--Georgia (Republic) 4. Economic assistance--Georgia (Republic) I. Papava, V. G. (Vladimir Georgievich)
HC415.19.E36 2011
338.94758--dc23
2011050195

Published by Nova Science Publishers, Inc. † New York

To Lana, Archil and George

CONTENTS

PREFACE

This book provides insight into the compelling evolution of Georgia's development and modern challenges. It analyzes the key tendencies that took place during the twenty years of reforming Georgia's economy.

INTRODUCTION

Georgia is one of the most ancient countries in the world (e.g., Lang, 1966; Metreveli, 1995) that has already made an exclusively correct decision to tie up its future with Europe and the West (Rondeli, 2001). This is very difficult and has a long way to go; its success can only be achieved by the gradual adoption of a European value system (Papava and Tokmazishvili, 2006). Indeed, such an approach concerns all spheres of life, inclusive of the financial and economic arrangement of the country (Khaduri, 2010a).

The relatively small area of Georgia (69,700 square kilometers) is distinguished by its extremely diverse landscape and natural-geographical conditions (e.g., Gachechiladze, 1995). This, as well as the interests of the territorial distribution of production in the former USSR, helped to form special features of economic development in Georgia and in other Soviet republics of the Caucasus (e.g., Adamescu and Silaev, eds., 1973; Asatiani, 2009a; Curtis, 1995; Herzig, 1999). No wonder that until now there have been many similarities among the post-Soviet countries of the region (Åslund, 2002, 2007; Khaduri, 2010b; Papava, 2010f, 2011a, 2011c; Silagadze and Tokmazishvili, 2009; Tokmazishvili and Silagadze, 2008).

A sufficiently developed industrial base was characteristic of the Soviet-Georgian economy, consisting of: metallurgy, the production of ferrous alloys; machine-building (agricultural machinery industry, aeronautical engineering, ship building) and the machine-tool industry; and the chemical industry. The agricultural produce and foodstuffs (primarily wine, mineral water, tea, and citrus fruit) were mainly exported beyond Georgia and were essentially in demand throughout the former USSR.

The collapse of the communist system in the Soviet society and the disintegration of the USSR led to a breakdown in cooperative relations among the enterprises of the former USSR and the disappearance of the system for supporting the consumption of these enterprises' products. The question of re-orienting foreign trade (Kaminski, 1996) became urgent. Most enterprises, on the whole of the former USSR, were incapable of meeting the demands of international competition. As a result of the divestment, the economies of each of these countries could not avoid the trend toward de-industrialization, with formation of a new phenomenon, the necroeconomy, only producing uncompetitive products due to their low quality and/or high price (Papava, 2001, 2002b, 2005c; Papava and Tokmazishvili, 2007).

Unfortunately, the situation in Georgia (as well as in some other post-Soviet countries) during the first years of its independence was exacerbated even more by conflicts (e.g., Antonenko, 2005; Birch, 1996; Coppieters, 2003; Cornell, 2001, 2002; Dragadze, 1999; Hunter, 1994; Nodia, 2000; O'Ballance, 1997). After Russia's war against Georgia in August 2008 (e.g., Cornell and Starr, eds., 2009), the economic situation in Georgia became more complicated (Kakulia, 2008b). The post-war status quo in Georgia created new challenges not only for Georgia (e.g., Beridze, 2009; Gegeshidze, 2009), but for its Western partners as well (e.g., Asmus, 2010; Bugajski, 2010; Charap and Welt, 2011; Popjanevski, 2011).

The origins these conflicts have had an especially negative effect on the economy of Georgia (Asatiani, 1998; Chkhartishivili, Gotsiridze and Kitsmarishvili, 2004); as a result of which, it has lost its potential for economic development (SRI, 2003).

As a result of these political, economic, and other factors, Georgia has found itself in a profound crisis that encompasses all spheres of its vital activity, leading to an abrupt slump in production, a high level of inflation, and a decline in the standard of living (Asatiani, 2009b; Gurgenidze, Lobzhanidze and Onoprishvili, 1994; Papava and Chikovani, eds., 1997; Slider, 1995).

Beginning in 1994-1995, thanks to actively carrying out an economic reform policy, trends toward stabilizing and improving the economy were observed in Georgia (Papava, 1995a, 1996a, 1996b, 1998, 1999; Papava and Chikovani, eds., 1997). These reforms were supported by the International Monetary Fund (IMF) and the World Bank programs.

From the mid-90s, ambitious projects for transporting Azerbaijan's hydrocarbon resources were implemented in Georgia (e.g., Chase, H., 2002; Kalicki, 2001; Maisaia, 2007; Papava, 2005e; Starr and Cornell, 2005). As a result, the role of Georgia has increased as a transport corridor in the Caucasus (Ismailov and Papava, 2006, pp. 107-109, 2008a, pp. 290-291, 2008b, pp. 77-79; Papava, 2005b, 2006a).

The "Rose Revolution" of November 2003 was an outcome associated with the Georgian people striving for the development of a democratic society and an improvement of the human rights record, a reduction of corruption, an enhancement of national economy and a qualitative improvement of the social conditions of life (e.g., Coppieters and Legvold, eds., 2005; Fairbanks, 2004; Karumidze and Wertsch, eds., 2005; Khutsishvili, ed., 2008; King, 2004; Miller, 2004; Welt, 2004). It is no surprise that the "Revolution" and its heroes, led by the present president of Georgia, Mr. Mikheil Saakashvili, have been supported by the administration of the US, the leadership of EU and its member states, and the whole civilized world.

With the passage of two years after the "Rose Revolution", the quite natural euphoria that had followed it, both inside and outside the country, has gradually diminished and has been replaced by a state of "sobering down", leading to a rather realistic evaluation of the results associated with post-revolution changes. It is important to note that such a sobering down from the "revolutionary drunkenness" has been taking place in Georgia rather more quickly than at oversees, quite understandably so: Georgian citizens have been experiencing all the "pleasures" of revolution all on their own whereas Georgia's international friends very often mistake what they would like to happen for what is really happening (Papava, 2006c). Nevertheless, even those analysts who have been a priori supportive of the revolutionary leaders could not turn a blind eye to some recent anti-democratic developments in Georgia (such as executives dominating judiciary) (Jones, 2006). There were even more sobering accounts as well (Kupchan, 2006, Mitchell, 2006).

From the very outset, the post-revolution political regime in Georgia was a kind of mixture of democratic and authoritarian elements (Nodia, 2005, p. 44-45). Such a hybrid of a regime is not a substantial novelty, but has always been a characteristic of many post-Communist countries (e.g., Bunce, 1999) that have avoided "color revolutions". After twenty years of its independence, the political regime in Georgia is still a combination of authoritarian rule and democracy (Gegeshidze, 2011; Leiashvili, 2010; Muskhelishvili, 2010). The model of "competitive authoritarianism" (Levitsky and Way, 2010) can also be applicable to describe the post-revolutionary development of Georgia (Lazarus, 2010).

While the crushing of the peaceful demonstrations in the Georgian capital, Tbilisi, in November 2007, appeared to be totally unexpected and, consequently, shocking to many of politicians in the West, these events were more or less predictable to the analysts (e.g., Areshidze, 2007; Lanskoy and Areshidze, 2008; Mitchell, 2008; Papava, 2008c). It was quite easy for those experts to foresee that sooner or later the officials of Tbilisi would show the rest of the world their real anti-democratic nature. Nonetheless, not all experts, even after November 2007, agree with the definition of the post-revolutionary political regime as being anti-democratic (e.g., Jones, 2008b).

After the five-day Russian-Georgian war in August 2008 (e.g., Cornell and Starr, eds., 2009), and in consideration of the global financial crisis (Papava, 2010f, 2011c), Georgia has come to face some new challenges (Papava, 2008f, 2009d; Tsiskarishvili, ed., 2009, 2010). These particularly include: liquidating economic damage caused by the war; avoiding a crisis in the banking sector; preventing any further growth of the relatively high inflation rate; and preserving the stability of the exchange rate of the national currency, the lari. Furthermore, it is of no less importance for the post-war Georgia to make a successful transition to the free trade regime proposed by the US and the EU. In general, under the process of globalization, Georgia faced new challenges for its economic development (Abesadze, 2011; Abesadze and Burduli, 2009; Achelashvili, 2011; Achelashvili and Achelashvili, 2008; Asatiani, 2007; Beridze, 2007; Burduli, 2007; Mekvabishvili, 2009; Papaphilippou, 2008; Papava and Chocheli, 2003; Samson, 2006, 2008).

To understand the main problems of Georgia's development and modern challenges it would be useful to analyze all those key tendencies that took place during the twenty years of reforming the independent Georgia's economy.

Chapter 1

First Steps and Initial Results of Reforms

1.1. Before Shock Therapy

The period from 1989, when the idea of national independence embraced the whole society, should be considered as a starting point for the post-Communist reform reasoning in Georgia (Suny, 1994, pp. 317–335). It became a turning point for both economists and those claiming to know economies, resulting in the creation of a number of interesting new concepts that were linked to the idea of economic independence (Papava, 1990). This stage of incipient reforms can conventionally be called *the stage of naive comprehension*.

The second stage of economic reform had started after the election of the Supreme Council in the autumn of 1990. At that time, several very important laws on economic reform were issued, although unfortunately they were implemented ineffectively. This stage of reform can, therefore, be considered *the stage of reform stagnation* (Papava, 1995a).

After the coup d'état of December 1991—January 1992 was *the stage of populist economic reform* began (Papava, and Beridze, 1994). At that time, the government transferred land and dwellings to people without compensation in order to enlist the easy support of the population. These redistributive policies caused substantial damage to the agricultural sector and house building. In particular, land privatization was carried out mechanically, and it practically ruined the necessary infrastructure for agricultural production (the system of supplying machinery, fertilizers, and other resources). Furthermore, without a legal basis for the private ownership of land, the efficiency of land tenure was very low. If the differentiation of rental payments for dwellings had been made according to location and amenities, the money received could have been accumulated for further housing development. This became impossible because of the overly hasty, free distribution of dwellings (Papava, 1992, pp. 97–101).

During this populist stage of economic reform, a method of Shock Therapy was used in Georgia at almost the same time as in Russia and in accordance with the Russian scenario. Was Georgia ready to apply this well-known approach to economic reform?

In order to answer this question, an important distinction of principle should be pointed out concerning the nature of the state. Thus, it turned out to matter a great deal whether countries were with or without their own independent statehood at the beginning of their reforms (Balcerowicz, 1995, p. 146; Milanovic, 1998, p, 3; Papava, 2000b, 2005d). To the first type belongs the countries of Eastern Europe, such as Poland, Hungary, Bulgaria, and so on; and to the second type belongs the newly created countries that followed the disintegration of the USSR, Yugoslavia, and Czechoslovakia. Among the latter countries, the legal successors of the original larger states are the only exceptions because they preserved almost all attributes of statehood. Thus, after the disintegration of the USSR, Russia was recognized as the legal successor of the USSR; retained Moscow as its capital; and preserved all the attributes of statehood, inheriting the institutions of the former Soviet Union (FSU). Hence, Russia can be classified with the group of post-Communist countries that had already possessed statehood. All other countries had to build up their own state institutions, often from almost nothing (to a certain extent, Ukraine and Belarus can be considered exceptions since, although formally lacking independent statehood, they were already members of the United Nations). Georgia was one of the countries facing this situation. Therefore, it had to simultaneously manage two major tasks: the need to build up the institutions of a new state and the process of transitioning from central planning to a market-type economy (Papava, 1996a, p. 252).

As is well known, the Shock Therapy method of economic reform was developed and first used in West Germany after World War II. New life was breathed into it in post-Communist Poland with the introduction of the "Balcerowicz Plan" in 1990 (Balcerowicz, 1994; Schaffer, 1992). The implementation of this approach to macroeconomic stabilization requires the active involvement of several different governmental institutions. To successfully apply the method of Shock Therapy in the absence of these crucial institutions is impossible, and any attempt to do so is doomed to failure. The experience of Georgia also supports the validity of this view. It is not difficult to demonstrate this. It is enough to elaborate what Shock Therapy means according to the so-called Balcerowicz Plan (considered today as the modem and already classical scheme of Shock Therapy) and then to study defects in its implementation when applied in Georgia, blindly imitating the reflections in the Russian "mirror" (Papava, 1996a, 1996b, 1999, 2002a, pp. 6–16).

1.2. UNACCOMPLISHED SHOCK THERAPY

The Shock Therapy generally assumes that a strict fiscal policy is being implemented. It entails the simultaneous adoption of measures concerned with price liberalization, a considerable reduction of the national budget deficit by canceling budgetary subsidies, and a stringent control over the population's money supply and income. The plan, developed by the former Polish finance minister, Leszek Balcerowicz, is considered an excellent modern example of the Shock Therapy method and is frequently favorably referred to by other transition economies. According to this plan (which is a classical scheme of the Shock Therapy modern approach in post-Communist countries), the following measures were simultaneously implemented in Poland from the very start:

1. Multiple increases of all types of prices; a deliberate, though it is hoped temporary, increase in inflation aimed at ensuring and maintaining market equilibrium;
2. Tough restrictions on the (real) incomes of the population;
3. Substantially increasing (nominal) interest rates and restrictions of the money supply;
4. Increasing the interest rates on deposits, aimed at stimulating the population to save;
5. Sharp cuts in national budget expenses by reducing government investments and by refusing to subsidize unprofitable enterprises any further;
6. Using issues of government bonds to help cover the national budget deficit;
7. Regulating the tax system and moving toward a more uniform, Western-type tax structure;

8. Introducing a common rate of exchange of the zloty to the dollar (involving a substantial initial devaluation) and ensuring zloty convertibility in the domestic market;
9. Introducing a common customs tariff in order to restrict imports and stimulate exports;
10. Providing social assistance to the population within the limits of government possibilities;
11. Eliminating monopoly positions and substantially withdrawing administrative intervention in enterprise activities.

The use of the Shock Therapy method began in Russia on January 2, 1992. It began in Georgia a month later. To explain how the Shock Therapy used in Georgia deviated from the Polish approach it is helpful to compare each step taken in Georgia with the corresponding item in the Balcerowicz Plan:

1. The reform of price formation started in Georgia as early as the spring of 1991 when free prices on some types of goods were introduced. If these changes were still of an exceptional character in 1991, were radical changes in the price formation system in Georgia by February 1992 (that is a month later than in Russia) there. Thus, the prices of one group of goods and services were liberalized, while the regulated prices of another group considerably increased. All this was aimed at balancing the market. If the consumer price index stood at 1.8 in 1991, it rose to 25 in 1992. At the same time, it is noteworthy that the regulated consumer prices increased sixty-eight times in 1992 in comparison with those of 1991 (100 times for bread, the main food product in Georgia). We can say that the first item of the Balcerowicz Plan was, on the whole, fulfilled in Georgia;
2. From 1992, the indexation of minimum wages and social security benefits began to be used in Georgia. In 1991 this indexation was carried out only once, but in 1992, in the process of liberalizing price formations, income indexation was performed six times. In 1991 the minimum wage and the average wage of employees increased in comparison to the previous year by 1.85 times and 1.26 times, respectively; and in 1992 compared with 1991 by 13.14 times and 17.94 times, respectively. True, there were no strict regulatory measures in Georgia to control increases in the wage fund (as was done in Poland when in, the case of a 2 percent overspending of the

wage fund, the penalty imposed on an enterprise was equal to 200 percent of this sum; and if the overspending was more than 2 percent the penalty was 300–500 percent of the corresponding sum), but the increases in wages and social security benefits lagged behind price increases. Thus, it can be considered that item two of the Balcerowicz Plan was also, to a certain extent, more or less fulfilled in Georgia;

3. In 1992 in comparison with 1991, the interest rate on deposits increased from 2 percent to 5 percent per annum, and the interest rate increased from 9 percent to 80 percent for ten-year deposits. Such an increase of interest rates was still far from reflective of the actual inflation rate. It should also be noted that it was generally impossible to restrict the money supply in Georgia in those days by increasing the interest rate because the country had no monetary system of its own; in Georgia, only the ruble of the already disintegrated USSR and the newly issued Russian ruble were in circulation.
4. In the summer of 1992 it was decided to double cash deposits on a deferred withdrawal basis. In particular, on July 25, the decision was taken to double cash deposits devalued by inflation on August 1. The population immediately responded by depositing more money in cash deposits. On August 1, a new decision was made to prolong the time available for placing money in cash deposits for doubling until August 10. After doubling, the additional money could be withdrawn after only a year, unless the money was to be used in the privatization process (which was, however, suspended at that time in Georgia). As it became rather difficult to receive the necessary quantity of bank notes from Russia in a timely way in the second half of 1992, the money accumulated in this way was paid out as wages and pensions, and this practically prevented the government from restricting the money supply. As a result, one can conclude that items three and four of the Balcerowicz Plan were not carried out in Georgia;
5. In 1992 the share of government investment in the total expenditure of the national budget was not reduced, and it varied 20–25 percent up to that year. The nominal amount of subsidies in 1992 compared with 1991 increased by about 5.1 times. However, in 1991 the share of subsidies in national budget expenditures amounted to the remarkably high level of 47 percent, and in 1992 this was cut back to 30.1 percent. Even so, this does not enable us to suggest that item five of the Balcerowicz Plan was realized in Georgia;

6. Government internal bonds were formally issued in 1992, but they were offered for sale only in autumn 1993 and mainly in order to convert bonds of the FSU into new Georgian bonds. As for the use of government bonds to meet the national budget deficit, it should be noted that this has not proved feasible during the next several years in Georgia. It is clear that item six of the Balcerowicz Plan was not implemented either;
7. A comprehensive reform of the tax system in accordance with the requirements of a market economy started as early as the spring of 1991. For this reason, item seven of the Balcerowicz Plan should be mainly considered as fulfilled in Georgia at that time although it should also be noted that further reform of the tax system is continuing constantly, as in many other countries of the world;
8. In 1992 there was no national currency in Georgia and so it was practically impossible to fulfill item eight of the Balcerowicz Plan;
9. In 1992, general customs tariffs were introduced at rates of 2 percent on imports and 8 percent on exports. Obviously, this policy did not favor either import restrictions or export stimulation. Thus, item nine of the Balcerowicz Plan was clearly not fulfilled in Georgia either;
10. It was already mentioned that in 1992, as in 1991, there was income indexation, albeit imperfectly applied and subject to lags. At that time, any type of assistance to families with low incomes was disregarded. That is to say, the social protection system did not differentiate by income level in a way that supported those with low real incomes. As a result, the real minimum wage in 1992 amounted to only 86 percent of that of 1991. Since, despite the income indexation in 1992, targeted assistance to the families most in need was inadequate, item ten of the Balcerowicz Plan was unfortunately not fulfilled;
11. In 1992, for the first time in Georgia, legal and governmental resolutions and decrees restricting monopolistic institutions and practices and promoting competition were issued although their effective implementation was significantly delayed. True, as early as 1991, the Soviet procedures for the centralized supply of resources to enterprises and final customers were disrupted and gradually abandoned, many elements of the system of state administrative interference in enterprise activity were still preserved. Hence, item eleven of the Balcerowicz Plan was also not carried out at that time.

Thus, in 1992 in Georgia, eight out of eleven items of the Balcerowicz Plan (that is, all except items one, two, and seven) were unfulfilled.

Also neglected were such important measures as the canceling, or at least serious restriction, of budgetary subsidies and tough restriction of the money supply. Many of those items were actually doomed to failure, above all, because there was no independent monetary system at that time in Georgia. In these conditions, implementing a defective variant of the Shock Therapy based only on price liberalization could hardly be expected to succeed. In other words, in the absence of corresponding governmental institutions, the transition to a market economy by using the Shock Therapy was practically impossible. In this situation it might have been much more effective to create the various institutions necessary for both pursuing reforms and constructing the Georgian state.

The populist stage of economic reform ended with the inevitable failure of the unaccomplished Georgian modification of the Shock Therapy, and this then gave rise to serious delays in their economic reform process.

1.3. Accumulation of Mistakes

The accumulation of mistakes stage includes 1993 and the first half of 1994 (Papava, 1995a). One factor resulting in delayed reforms was outside the economic sphere, whereas another factor explained delays in terms of basic mistakes of economic policy. The economy of Georgia (and not only the economy) was prepared neither for the full-scale military operations that started in Abkhazia in the summer of 1992 nor for the civil war that intensified in the autumn of 1993. These events seriously strained the national budget, and it proved impossible to get the budget approved in advance by the normal manner in 1993–94. The only possible source to cover the resulting deficits were money emissions.

Both in consequence of a general amnesty announced in the winter of 1992 and later on through its participation in military operations (as a country without an army), the crime situation in Georgia worsened so much that it became too dangerous to conduct most economic activity. As a result, many businessmen left their native land, and this accelerated the outflow of capital. At the same time, undisguised robbery was replaced by racketeering, also not conducive to successful business development. These criminal elements could not usually manage to accumulate wealth. The reason for this is that the overwhelming majority of these people were drug addicts or had links with the drug trade, and so there was substantial leakage of stolen property to the neighboring countries from where the drugs illegally penetrated into Georgia.

In late 1992 and early 1993 the most important policy mistake occurred. The government, for some reason, did not expect that it would receive additional banknotes from Moscow, and it, therefore, brought the temporary banknotes of Georgia, the Georgian coupon of the National Bank of Georgia (NBG), into circulation (Gotsiridze, 2008, p.164-166). Unfortunately, representatives of the Georgian Government and the NBG were unable to take the new currency seriously, sometimes revealing contemptuous attitudes towards it. This had a decisive impact on the already serious devaluation process under way. Basically, the nature of the mistake was the illusion that it was economically expedient for Georgia to remain temporarily or even permanently within the proposed "ruble zone". As a result of this unfortunate illusion, the coupon became the sole legal tender of payment only in July–August 1993 when Russia carried out a partial currency reform of its own and withdrew the FSU's ruble from circulation. This act made it clear that Georgia would be obliged to introduce its own currency.

Uncontrolled credit emissions were the foundation of the inflationary process in Georgia. Attempts to solve agricultural problems (e.g., the procurement of agricultural products in autumn 1993 and carrying out essential agricultural work in spring 1994) from a budget that had been practically nonexistent since the autumn of 1993 had resulted in initially unreported budgetary emissions that finally ruined the financial system of the country. Georgia developed a hyperinflationary spiral, with the inflation rate proceeding at some 60–70 percent per month from 1993 until autumn 1994. In the long run, this money was not, unfortunately, used for agricultural purposes. In conditions of such high inflation, the coupon could not perform the normal function of sustaining commercial turnover because the real value of the coupon supply was constantly falling. Other things being equal, this promoted wider use of the ruble instead of the coupon as a means of payment (Gurgenidze, Lobzhanidze and Onoprishvili, 1994).

In 1991–92, the foundations of a system of informal relations, which are characteristic of low-income countries (Adams, and Fitchett, eds., 1992), were laid down in Georgia.

The incorrect policy of the NBG towards restricting cash circulation (which gave rise, contrary to common sense, to restrictions on the withdrawal of coupons from the banking system) resulted in substantial discrepancies between cash and non-cash monetary values. This further restricted the circulation of the coupon. Also, state-owned commercial banks tolerated excessive overdrafts, promoting hidden credit emissions. Subsidized prices on bread, gas, electricity, and transport gave the budget additional loading and also promoted budgetary emissions.

A serious error that allowed the "unique Georgian" clearing system to be consolidated was perpetrated in Georgia's foreign trade policy. Barter was considered the only way to receive gas from Turkmenistan. The prices of both Turkmen gas and a lot of poor-quality goods produced in Georgia were artificially overcharged. According to the "innovators" of such an approach, this would result in the creation of an environment for Georgian enterprises that stimulated their activity. It should be mentioned that such an environment for producing goods of poor quality had really been created. At the same time, this production had to be purchased by government. In the absence of a proper budget, however, this operation could be only partially carried-out and, even then, only by means of money emission (which also promoted inflation). Most of this production was taken from enterprises by the government by using a form of the state order system, with guarantees to pay corresponding prices in the future. Using the system of state orders required a complicated system of quotas and licensing. When receiving debts from different foreign countries and international organizations, the interest rates and prices on goods bought with the help of credits were artificially increased in some cases, and the credits received were partly used in less important directions. Needless to say, this put these enterprises in a difficult financial situation and resulted in the formation of a non-payment network that was difficult to stop within the country. It became impossible for the government to collect the full volume of goods within the country to fulfill the barter commodity exchange agreed with Turkmenistan. In recent years, the existing difficulties with the Azerbaijan transport route (the blocking of the railway line passing through Chechnya) at first complicated, and then made impossible, to normally transport goods assembled by the government to Turkmenistan. As a result of these difficulties and mistakes, Georgia's debt to Turkmenistan amounted to about half a billion US dollars over two years. The country's total external debt rose to one billion US dollars.

Ignoring the interests of enterprise workers and employees had effectively impeded the privatization process in 1992–93 and held up the restructuring of enterprises into joint-stock companies.

Much of this is behind the energy crisis, associated with the use of credits for purposes other than the intended ones; non-payment for the real cost of power resources (in other words, absurdly low domestic prices); chronic irresponsibility in regards to technical norms that made it impossible to carry out not only capital renewal, but even routine repairs and maintenance; and the constant theft of power equipment containing copper (including wire) to sell in Turkey (e.g., Natelauri, 2007). All the aforementioned factors, including the energy crisis, gave rise to an unprecedented collapse of production.

Moreover, given the general state of disarray in both national and enterprise-level accounting, it became impossible to obtain the full information on firms and their activities. This, in its turn, artificially exaggerated the already apparent decline in the major macroeconomic indicators and, at the enterprise level, facilitated firms' efforts to hide their tax liabilities.

This stage of economic reform was characterized by extremely imperfect recordings of foreign economic activities, inefficient customs procedures, extensive commodity stock waste, a decline in the economic role of normal wages, unrecorded expansion of the shadow economy, and uses of humanitarian aid for purposes other than those intended. Overall, the picture of the Georgian economy was exceedingly bleak.

1.4. "Minimal Shock with Maximum Therapy"

At the beginning of 1994, Georgia's Head of State, Eduard Shevardnadze, initiated the preparation of an anti-crisis program for macroeconomic stabilization and systemic change. In the spring of 1994, the program was initiated, and this made a good start to the *correction of mistakes stage,* committed during the earlier stages of the economic reform process.

This new stage of economic reform was also characterized by problems of a noneconomic nature. By spring 1994, the hostilities in Abkhazia had already come to an end. True, this fact had a positive influence on the economy as a whole, but it also gave rise to a new problem: social protection of internally displaced persons (IDP), a heavy burden on the national budget.

Law-enforcement institutions intensified the fight against criminals in order to improve the situation. Definite positive results were achieved, but the country still had a long way to go to solve the problem. Many enterprises, for instance, were afraid to undertake high levels of production for fear of being robbed by organized (including semi-official) and other criminal elements.

From the spring of 1994, the government gradually changed its attitude toward the coupon. According to the standard policy of the IMF, it was ready to assist any country that had its own currency and whose government did its best to strengthen it. If Georgia stayed within the ruble zone the IMF would undoubtedly prefer to work with Russia, the country issuing the ruble. This fact undermined the positions of those in Parliament and the Government (the Speaker of Parliament or Minister of Finance) supporting the ruble zone since they would have had to openly advocate the requirement to regard the Russian ruble as the sole legal tender. Conversely, it assisted those in power who, from the very beginning, realized that the Georgian economy had no prospects without its own national currency. Interestingly, in 1994, a noble but perhaps hopeless experiment was already going on in Kutaisi where the city authorities were supporting the coupon, the only region of Georgia to do so. All of this, together with the relative stabilization of the Georgian coupon and worsening depreciation of the ruble, encouraged the population to take the coupon more seriously.

Uncontrolled monetary emissions became impossible, owing to the increasing firmness of the NBG authorities. In the autumn of 1994, under obvious pressure of the IMF, the Bank cancelled the prevailing restrictions on the withdrawal of cash from the banks. As a result, cash and non-cash money values drew considerably closer to each other.

From late 1994, as per the advice of the IMF, the NBG started regulating the banking system by using classical methods widely used elsewhere in the world. Apart from solving other problems, this prevented the state-owned commercial banks from continuing to work in overdraft conditions. Also, from the second half of 1994, the corporatization process of the state-owned commercial banks had started.

According to the program worked out with the IMF in September 1994, the prices of gas and electricity were raised to world levels, the price of bread had increased 285 times (!), and subway fares and tariffs on other municipal services greatly increased. There was a wage increase for those employed in activities financed by the budget, and pensions and social welfare payments were also increased, but these increases considerably lagged behind the price rise. This enabled a great reduction in the budgetary subsidies needed to cover the discrepancies between consumer and producer prices, or between producer prices and actual costs. A substantial strengthening of the Georgian coupon rate thus followed. Whereas one dollar was worth 5.3 million coupons before the price rise on bread, one dollar was already valued at 2.4 million coupons after the price rise. This process continued; at the end of 1994 the price of bread increased again by 40 percent and as a result a stable coupon exchange rate was established (one dollar = 1.3 million coupons) (Wang, 1998; Wellisz, 1996).

Unfortunately, Georgia could not manage a full recovery of money for gas or electricity. However, if enterprises and the population did not pay for their gas and electricity supplies, or paid only negligible sums, the price of bread was almost fully paid by the population. Delays in enforcing these payments encouraged a more skeptical attitude toward the coupon by economic agents: trade organizations, enterprises, and banks delayed corresponding money transfers and conducted speculative operations in the currency market, sustaining significant losses in the process. Starting from 1995, when the coupon rate became stable, a timely withdrawal of these sums was prevented not only by the sluggishness of the banks, but also by some local authorities temporarily using these sums in order to settle the problems of their local budgets.

Also, the pseudo-protection of enterprises by some representatives of government, and the often groundless fears of the population about interruptions of supply, meant that payment enforcement by cessation of deliveries—the normal method in market-type economies—was not achieved. Gas supply to the population of Tbilisi only stopped in January 1995. A stricter policy to recover the cost of bread was carried out and achieved step-by-step in the first and second quarters of 1995.

The impossibility of collecting the full cost of gas and electricity also meant that the government could not revise the corresponding prices because of the general commitments on reform. The dollar prices of gas and electricity increased every month as a result of the coupon's strengthening. This led to an artificial increase in the product cost, having an adverse affect, first of all, on industrial enterprises. Following a review of its commitments to the IMF, the Georgian government revised coupon prices downward. In particular, since April 1995, the cost of gas has been reduced by 35 percent and the cost of electricity by 25 percent. At the same time, the Government of Georgia (GoG) refused to purchase gas after June 1995. Instead, purchases had to be undertaken by the immediate consumers, namely by Sakenergo (Georgian state energy company), big industrial enterprises, and municipalities. To enable these direct purchases of gas by consumers to take place, the aforementioned Georgian clearing system was, in effect, annulled.

All of this resulted in the requirement to terminate quotas and simplify licensing to be put on the agenda, and this process soon started. The system of quotas was completely annulled with effect from June 1, 1995, and licensing was preserved for only a limited list of goods. Order was also re-established in borrowing and using debts, building on the practices established in connection with Georgia's first loans from the IMF and the World Bank. In December 1994, Georgia received the first tranche of a Systemic Transformation Facility (STF) (approximately 39 million US dollars) from the IMF.

After a two-year interval, approval of the national budget by Parliament at the beginning of 1995 can be considered a very important step towards establishing order in Georgia's financial system . The real significance of this budget is in that emissions of credit and monetary emissions themselves were not used to balance the budgetary revenues and expenditures. In 1995, only 47 percent of the expenditures of the national budget were covered by taxes, and the remaining 53 percent had to be covered through the monetization of wheat and flour received as humanitarian aid (mobilizing proceeds of sales in the national budget). In that way, an unbalanced budget could be balanced without money emission. It was achieved through the help of donor countries and institutions promoting reforms in Georgia. Unfortunately, the planned macroeconomic indicators for the first two quarters were not achieved, though the actual results were improving considerably month by month.

With the support and efforts of the IMF, the majority of the countries to which Georgia's debt of approximately one billion US dollars was owed had agreed to a debt rescheduling. This allowed the IMF to allocate the second credit tranche of the STF at the end of June 1995 (approximately 44 million US dollars) and the stand-by credit (approximately 113 million US dollars). All of this was expected to create the conditions for Georgia to preserve financial stability, to carry out currency reform, and to place the *lari* (national currency) into circulation, avoiding the errors previously committed by the government in connection with the coupon (Kakulia, 2008a; Papava, 1996a, 1996b, 1999; Wang, 1998; Wellisz, 1996).

The exchange rate of the national currency was expected to remain unaltered until the end of 1995. After July of 1995, the price of bread increased by 7 percent on average, whereas the wages of budget sector employees increased, on average, by 50 percent. In autumn 1995, the liberalization of bread prices was planned. This was expected to become possible as a result of the planned dissolution of the government's monopoly in this sphere.

From July 1, 1995, the minimum monthly wage for those employed in the budget sector was just $2.69 and the maximum $12.69. These figures are, of course, very low although one should recall that at the beginning of September 1994, the minimum wage was less than ten cents, and the maximum a little more than a dollar (all evaluated using the then prevailing exchange rate, without adjustment for purchasing power parity).

From the point of view of sectoral development, the reforms in Georgia have been implemented most vigorously in the healthcare system where the project for reform was elaborated in close cooperation with experts of the

World Bank. A gradual transition to paid medical service and establishing a system of medical insurance had been started in the healthcare sphere.

In May 1994, the Head of State issued a decree according to which enterprise personnel were given precedence in the corporatization process. This speeded up the process. At the same time, the process of privatization, by means of direct purchases, was also encouraged. During 1995 in Georgia, as in many other former Communist countries, the process of using vouchers in privatization began: part of the social property is distributed to people free of charge (Silagadze and Beridze, 1996). The approach is justified by the necessity to give everyone a fair chance to acquire assets in the course of privatization (Papava, 1992, pp. 92–97, 1995b).

The success of the Shock Therapy in 1994–1995 rests on the paradox: “The Worse, the Better”. Therefore, such a situation might be classified as “Minimal Shock with Maximum Therapy”. If there is a big question mark over the country’s future and its ability to survive, there must be no doubt whether the Shock Therapy method is really needed: the country has no choice under such circumstances, and positive results are almost guaranteed. Such a situation might be classified as “Minimal Shock with Maximum Therapy” or the “Soft Big Bang” (Papava, 2005c, pp. 23–24; 2005d, pp. 85–86).

Chapter 2

Role of the International Monetary Fund in the Transformation of the Georgian Economy before the "Rose Revolution"

2.1. Before Starting Reforms with Support of the IMF

After regaining Georgia's independence, perhaps of the greatest importance was whether or not the healthy and truly professional people coming to power would be able to push economic reforms in the right direction. To be victorious, any good idea needs serious political and financial support. However, for a country like Georgia, so weakened by exhausting military actions, the mobilization of domestic financial resources turned out to be a very hard, if not a practically unsolvable, problem. International financial and various other institutions, such as the IMF, the World Bank, and the EU, had a great role in addressing this issue. Obviously, of these institutions, particular stress should be placed on the IMF, owing to the coordinating functions that the international financial system has conferred on it.

Naturally, economic science has to answer the question of what changes should be made in the economic basis of society during the course of a post-Communist transformation and, especially, how these changes should be made. Unluckily, it turned out that economists had not been prepared to ensure scientific support of the transformation process: there was no universal economic theory on the basis for which an essentially right economic policy could have been developed for all post-Communist states (Stiglitz, 1996, p. 3). Under such circumstances, in view of, at best, sound professional intuition of an economist giving advice, any economist who makes judgments on the basis of general principles of economic theory and the experience of market-oriented reforms implemented in other countries in transition can be regarded as optimally close to what is desired (Adams and Brock, 1993, p. XIII).

In the early phases of transition to a market economy, the GoG was tempted to solve the hardest problems of transition on its own. In a number of instances, members of the government would seek “free advice” of either their compatriots who had temporarily returned to their homelands, or foreign charlatans “transiting” through the country (Papava, 2003b, p. 6). Very often these latter, ostensibly with the purpose of pushing economic reforms and improving the hard social conditions of the people, would attempt to import millions of dollars into the country, earned by drug trafficking, illegal manufacturing of or trade in weapons, and so on—in other words, “dirty” money. In that case, the mechanism of laundering such money is to compel the government to issue financial guarantees for borrowing huge credit resources (tens and hundreds of millions, even billions of dollars). As a rule, such transactions are implemented through obviously suspicious mediators.

Given the ways by which dirty money is generally made and, more importantly, the sort of people who are usually involved in making such money, a natural question arises: if dirty money can only be made by cheating and robbing people, how can it be expected that, in the course of “laundering” such dirty money, the magnates who make that money will become honest overnight? Undoubtedly, I believe a crook is not likely to ever give up wrongdoing, whatever the circumstances may be.

It must be noted that in the early 1990s, Georgia did have some attempts to use financial guarantees in order to attract some dirty money. The NBG and the Ministry of Finance (MoF) issued many of letters of guarantee for many billions of dollars. Further developments showed that this was a wrong way to get credits. Furthermore, the guarantees themselves became the subject of international speculation. If the IMF had not interfered, Georgia’s financial situation could have been even more difficult.

At the time when Georgia joined the IMF and the World Bank, the number of their members equaled 170. The quota (vote) for Georgia in these institutions amounts to 0.08 percent.

As was noted above, at the time of Georgia’s joining the IMF and the World Bank, the world nations had already maintained financial order, which was actually the only lawful way to receive monetary support in the form of "clean" money. Maintaining such an order is the only choice for any country, including Georgia, which had opted for civilized forms of economic development.

The first IMF mission arrived in Georgia in November 1991. The objective for this first visit was to get familiar with local circumstances. After that, during each successive visit, the IMF mission would leave the Georgian government with their recommendations on how to accomplish macroeconomic stability in the country. Unfortunately, governmental officials in charge at the time (with rare exceptions) had paid little attention to both those recommendations and their authors (Gotsiridze and Kandelaki, 2001; Papava, 1995a). As a result, the country's financial system came to a state of complete disorder. In 1993 and 1994 Georgia did not have any parliament-adopted national budget; the constitutional and legislative process was practically nonexistent; poor quality of adopted laws and, what really matters, extensive tax privileges to a wide range of organizations (such as churches, theaters, etc.) made it impossible to raise fiscal revenues, even to a minimum level; government officials' attitude toward a temporary national currency (the coupon) was that of sustainable nihilism; and the NBG's self-indulgent monetary policy and repeated issue of huge amounts of Georgian currency (aimed, for example, at covering agricultural production costs) caused hyperinflation. In consequence, in 1993 and 1994 the rate of inflation reached 50–70 percent a month (Gurgenidze, Lobzhanidze and Onoprishvili, 1994).

2.2. Main Achievements

In 1994, President Eduard Shevardnadze initiated an "anti-crisis program," a key premise of which was to advance relationships with the IMF to an essentially new level. Specifically, the status of the IMF recommendations was upgraded from "desirable" to "mandatory". This fact was to bear very positive economic consequences.

Given this, for the facilitation of analysis, the IMF activities in Georgia could be split into two phases.

During *phase one,* that is, in 1991–1994, the IMF would provide the Georgian government with important recommendations although this "naughty child" would take no notice of those; during *phase two,* that is, since 1994 to the present time, the IMF recommendations have been considered mandatory although very often it has been hard to implement those recommendations and, above all, they have not always been commensurate with the true aspirations of some governmental officials.

The most important consequences of the IMF activities in Georgia are that the country has succeeded in building up its own financial system and achieved macroeconomic stability.

More specifically, one has to place stress on the following achievements (Papava, 1995a; 1996a; 1999; 2003a, pp. 9–12, 2003b, p.7–9; Wang, 1998; Wellisz, 1996):

1. The legal framework of the country's financial system regulating market-based budgetary and monetary processes has been developed and adopted;
2. As a result of restrictive monetary policy, the NBG's hyper-inflation was curbed; this made the successful implementation of the currency reform possible (the Georgian coupon and the Russian ruble were removed from circulation, and a newly introduced stable national currency, the lari, was granted the status of a legal tender);
3. The process of price liberalization has practically been completed (the hardest part of which was the release of bread prices);
4. As of 1995, Parliament would adopt national budgets practically not later than the beginning of each successive year;
5. A two-tier banking system was formed by which functions of the NBG and commercial banks have been delineated; in addition, the NBG has adopted a regulatory framework for commercial banks on the basis of which the NBG controls the banking system;
6. The process of privatization of all former government-owned banks has been completed;
7. Full liberalization of external trade has been achieved (inclusive of the encouraging of exports via lifting VAT and customs duties as well as releasing external trade from all non-tariff regulating mechanisms) (Papava and Beridze, 1996/1997);
8. Foreign debts have been restructured, and conditions for the servicing of those debts have been established; Georgia has acquired the image of a country that is able to pay back its debts.

It must also be noted that the IMF took an active position with respect to the support from the World Bank, one of the key requirements of which was to give priority to the budgetary spending for education and health care. It is also noteworthy that the IMF has provided sustainable support to the World Bank programs in Georgia, the primary objective of which was to implement structural reforms of the Georgian economy.

In 1996 and 1997, as a result of the IMF operations in Georgia, both a high rate of economic growth and a very moderate rate of inflation were observed. In the meantime, macroeconomic stability is the most important condition, without which it is impossible to implement any more-or-less significant investment project in a country. Aggressive measures recommended by the IMF for forming a favorable environment for investments, under other equal conditions, are also of great importance for the realization of the Silk Road reinstating plan (Shevardnadze, 1999).

Of course, this list could be extended, but perhaps the most important outcome from the cooperation between Georgia and the IMF is the fact that, at least, there has been a reduction of "popular amateurishness," a phenomenon that unluckily could be repeatedly observed in the government's actions (e.g., "swelling" foreign debts by using artificially increased clearing prices; imposing special taxes on local producers and importers of grains and flour, and official attempts to get the IMF's respective authorizations; announcing that the government was going to tax amnesty to tax evaders and presenting a relevant program of actions to the IMF; "distorting" the country's financial system by establishing a Ministry of Tax Revenues and weakening the MoF "for the benefit" of certain governmental officials; utilizing commercial bank loans for the purpose of implementing the national budgetary plans and thereby interfering with the process of forming a stock market; and directly distributing different food products or rendering certain services instead of paying unpaid pensions, etc.). Without insistent pressure on the part of the IMF, for example, distribution of flour in place of paying pensions (and other similar actions) in some parts of Georgia would have become a general rule rather than a single fact, which sooner or later would have brought down the national economy and finances. The key "achievement" of such "popular amateurishness" consisted in the gradual worsening of relationships between Georgia and the IMF.

2.3. Main Failures

One of the leading economists of our time, the former vice president and former senior economist of the World Bank, Joseph Stiglitz, wrote that during the sessions devoted to the fiftieth anniversary of the Bretton Woods institutions (the World Bank and the IMF), one could repeatedly hear remarks such as: “Fifty years is enough” (Stiglitz, 1999, p. F577).

Naturally, everyone makes mistakes, and the IMF is not an exception: it makes mistakes too, both in general (e.g., de Gregorio, Eichengreen, Ito and Wyplosz, 1999) and with respect to particular countries (e.g., Gomulka, 1995, pp. 14–19). Unfortunately, Georgia could not escape the IMF’s mistakes as well (Papava, 2003a, pp. 27–47, 2003b, pp. 9–24).

Mistakes made by the IMF in Georgia vary both by their nature and their implication. One has to note, however, that some of those mistakes have a very general character; in other words, they have been made by the Fund not only while working in Georgia, but also in a broader context in other countries as well.

One also has to note that the Georgian governmental team that had to negotiate with the IMF in the earliest phase of relationships, practically had neither any experience with conducting such talks nor a good understanding of IMF procedures, a situation the members of the IMF missions would take advantage of either consciously (perhaps to simplify a task) or unintentionally (which is more probable), but in all cases, quite skillfully (as it seems from the present angle). In each particular case, in order to get each successive tranche, the Georgian party had to assume such commitments, the implementation of which, in given time limits (actually, as a rule, in a very short period of time), would be very difficult; at the moments of accepting such commitments, the government was not always confident about how difficult the task of implementing those commitments could have been. Reformers, repeatedly resorting to unpopular measures while dealing with certain problems, as a rule, would point at the recommendations of the IMF and other financial institutions, for which reason, the public in general, and businesspeople in particular, started strongly disapproving of those institutions.

At the same time, it must be noted that all requirements of the IMF have officially been fixed as statements of the government (rather than IMF requirements). As a result, in each disputable situation, the IMF experts, as a rule, would remind the government that these have been the commitments taken on by the government; that is, it has been the government’s position rather than that of the IMF. Also, one has to take into account the fact that in all cases, in order to carry out the agreements reached between the Georgian government and the IMF, it was the governmental team conducting the negotiations that would assume a full and exclusive responsibility for the measures to be carried out. Furthermore, not all members of such teams (first of all, those responsible for fiscal and budgetary issues) would agree to assume such a responsibility; some members of the government (and Parliament) had, at best, never understood (and perhaps even never wanted to understand) what it meant to carry out commitments to the IMF.

Moreover, one has to take into account circumstances, such as inclusion in the negotiating teams, of certain governmental officials (at their request) who had a very poor reputation among the IMF staff. Ultimately, this would bring about a rejection of issues raised by such people, however justified, from the standpoint of reforms, they may be. However, this would happen quite seldom because more often during such meetings they would raise obviously erroneous and even completely unacceptable questions, negatively affecting the reputation of the person representing the government as well as that of the governmental agency that was directly represented by such a person. In all such instances, the negative reputation of such persons would have a negative impact on public opinion in regards to the IMF-supported programs as well. Furthermore, individual politicians, officials, and ordinary citizens would get a false impression that the members of the governmental team involved in the official negotiations with the Fund lacked competency and consistency, and that they were unable to find the right arguments during their discussions with the IMF; however, if they could have taken over, the success would have been very quick and definite. Under such circumstances, without a firm reform-oriented attitude of both the President's and Parliament's leadership, Georgia would never achieve those results that we discussed above and that were achieved owing to the IMF's extensive support.

Perhaps in the context of such an experience of cooperation with the IMF, it is easier to understand which mistakes could have been avoided in the very beginning and which mistakes were completely unavoidable.

Before starting to review those mistakes, it is essential to give some explanations that may facilitate our understanding as to the substance for most of them. Specifically, because the majority of mistakes made by the IMF in Georgia are related to taxation, we must formulate those criteria, or more specifically, we must give those characteristics of the taxation system on the basis by which the nature and the meaning of each mistake can be evaluated.

An ideal taxation system should be built on the following key principles (Chappell, 1990, pp. 41–44):

1. *Simplicity:* The primary goal of the system must be that each individual could understand independently, that is, without any assistance of tax experts, all issues related to taxes;
2. *Plainness:* Taxation should be based on a single flat rate;

3. *Rate*: A tax rate should depend on a required amount of receivable incomes; at the same time, the rate should be high enough to discourage taxpayers from tax evasion;
4. *Universality*: Taxes and tax rates should be universal throughout the country, and no exemptions and privileges should be allowed. At the same time, certain governmental support may be provided, for example, to the disabled. However, such support should be in the form of special social programs and grants rather than tax exemptions;
5. *Comprehensiveness:* Taxes should be imposed on both incomes and expenses;
6. *Evenhandedness:* Taxes should not distort different forms of saving and ideally should not make any distinction between spending and saving.

Naturally, there is no ideal taxation system in the real world; however, its significance for the estimation of strengths and weaknesses of existing taxation systems is obvious.

2.3.1. Political Mistakes

While reviewing the criticism of the IMF activities, we noted that the Fund often disregards the history, cultural traditions, and national peculiarities of the countries in which it operates. The same mistake could be observed from the very beginning of the IMF operations in Georgia. In particular, we are referring to the Fund's advice to the Georgian government to stay in the "ruble zone" and not to introduce a national currency. This advice was given to the Georgian government in February 1992.

It would hardly be possible to completely understand the motives that drove the Fund to give such advice. At best, we have to presume that it wanted to be cautious about irritating certain still influential and imperialistically ambitious forces in Russia. Perhaps it was for this reason that the IMF was not hurrying to make a violent intrusion into the monetary domain of the disintegrating empire. However, if we remember that this advice was applicable to the rest of the former Soviet republics too, except for the Baltic states (Estonia, Latvia, and Lithuania), we may presume that the Fund would have preferred to work with one single issuer of the national currency rather than with twelve issuers, enabling the Fund to establish one mission instead of twelve, and thereby save some money. It is noteworthy, in this regard, that only those countries that have introduced their own currencies are eligible for IMF credits (e.g., Lavigne, 1995, p. 207).

Anders Åslund tried to explain the IMF's desire to preserve the ruble zone by the fact that the IMF was skeptical about the technical abilities of the newly independent states that emerged after the disintegration of the FSU to introduce their own currencies, believing that a good currency reform should have been preceded by a country's preparation for genuine macroeconomic stabilization (which, we believe, is completely impossible if the country is out of its own monetary mechanisms of macroeconomic regulation). As a result, the IMF was afraid of being blamed for possible failures of the newly introduced national currencies (Åslund, 1995, Ch. 4).

Opponents who were radically critical about the IMF considered that this mistake was a result of the fact that the IMF and the governments of the donor countries (members of the IMF) had failed to understand (or even had never tried to understand) the political situation that had emerged after the disintegration of the USSR; that they had failed (or even had never wanted to) to analyze the history of that imperialistic nation; that they had failed to realize the national and cultural features of countries such as Georgia, which had driven Georgia and other former Soviet republics to strive after real national independence. We believe that such a judgment is obviously exaggerated, and the reason for the IMF's behaving in the above-described manner was that the IMF had been cautious about Russia.

One must presume that without the stringent steps taken by Russia itself, as a result of which it ceased providing Georgia and other former Soviet republics with Russian rubles, the IMF would never have hurried to change its attitude toward the ruble zone. Here, we must remember that the NBG raised a question of introducing a national currency at the very first meeting with the IMF mission (in November 1991), having presented all necessary calculations and samples of national currency bills and coins. The NBG requested the IMF to help Georgia prepare for currency reform. Unfortunately, this request was not taken into consideration. One has to presume that the Fund's refusal, in addition to what was stated above, was motivated by the outburst of military actions in Georgia in the winter of 1991–1992.

In 1993, Georgia was practically unprepared to introduce its own currency. To a certain extent, this was prompted by the actions on the part of the IMF. However, it would be unfair to put the blame completely on the IMF because at the time, firstly, the Georgian government had never paid any attention to the IMF recommendation and, secondly, it had been under an illusion that it would have been possible to stay within the ruble zone for a certain period of time. Such an attitude, under other equal conditions, was clearly reflected in the government's extremely nihilistic position on the temporary Georgian currency, the coupon.

The IMF corrected (if we are allowed to use this word) this mistake in the fall of 1995 when, in line with a plan coordinated with the IMF and owing to its financial support, a currency reform was implemented. In other words, a new Georgian currency, the lari, was introduced.

Another big mistake in relation to Georgia was made by the IMF while dealing with a problem of identifying the successors of foreign debts and assets of the FSU.

In 1993, Russia and Georgia signed an agreement (known as a "Zero Scenario"), according to which Russia would become a successor of all foreign debts and assets of the FSU. For some reason, the text of the signed agreement did not contain provisions (more precisely, they were "dropped" from it) about the fate of both the Diamond Stocks of the FSU and the deposits of the Georgian individuals and entities in the Vnesheconombank of the USSR, which had been included in the original, initialed version of the agreement.

Unfortunately, during the subsequent seven years, the IMF constantly refrained from intervening in this disputable question although, because of the aforementioned difference between the signed and the initialed versions, Georgia would refuse to ratify the agreement. Meanwhile, according to the IMF procedures, this might have become a serious impediment to the IMF's extending credits to Russia because of the failure of Russia to settle its foreign debts.

After the end of this seven-year period, however, when the question of restructuring Georgia's debts to Russia (accumulated after the disintegration of the USSR) was put on the agenda, under the pressure of the Russian government and with the silent consent of the IMF, Georgia had to ratify the agreement, thereby putting a question mark over the possibility of serving justice and reinstating in the agreement the aforementioned provisions that had been "dropped" from the initialed text of the agreement.

2.3.2. Methodical Mistakes

Immediately after gaining independence, Georgia faced the problem of establishing numerous governmental institutions. A taxation system was one of those institutions: there was a need to adopt a new tax law, establish tax and customs offices, and ensure their staffing, in spite of the scarcity of qualified human resources (e.g., Berulava, 2010). One has to remember that, by then, the people of Georgia and particularly its developing businesses had no experience and tradition of paying taxes under the conditions of a market economy, and a sense of responsibility in this regard had been practically nonexistent. In other words, neither taxpayers accurately knew what and how they should pay, nor the government knew what and how it should collect. Naturally, under such circumstances, the taxation system could not avoid certain shortcomings and mistakes and, as an immediate effect of it, corruption as well (it is noteworthy that at the time, corruption was based on the traditions and experiences accumulated during the Soviet period).

Elementary logic requires that at the initial stage of transition to a market economy, the taxation system should be as simple as possible. On the whole, the IMF shares such a belief, too. Specifically, one of the IMF experts, Leif Muten, notes that the taxation system must be simple enough in the course of transition to a market economy (Tanzi, ed., 1993, Ch. 8).

The improvement of the taxation system must be carried out gradually, in line with the improvement of tax education and the development of taxpayer habits.

In view of this logic, it was a complete mistake to replace the turnover tax with the VAT from the very beginning, when the financial system of independent Georgia was still in its embryonic state. The point is that in Communist-type economies, the turnover tax, by its nature, is not a tax at all; instead, it is a government-established difference between a unit cost and a producer's price (or wholesale price) (e.g., Tanzi, ed., 1993, Ch. 7, 1994, Ch. 6). As to the VAT, its economic contents, calculating methodologies, and mechanisms of collection are too complicated for mass application (e.g., Ebrill, Keen, Bodin and Summers, 2001). By far, imposing any other indirect tax, the administration of which would be much simpler, would be more justified. The sales tax (or the turnover tax based on a value-added rate) is a good example because it has to be paid at the final stage of procurement; for this reason, the mechanism of imposing this tax is quite transparent to a taxpayer and, at the same time, it is quite easy for a tax collector to administrate. This practice was applied, for example, in Romania (Tanzi, ed., 1994, Ch. 6).

One has to admit, though, owing to its economic nature, the VAT is more acceptable than the sales tax because, in the case of the former, all phases of business are subject to taxation and, therefore, the burden of taxation lies on all such phases. Despite this, in the United States, a country with long and rich tax traditions, the sales tax is still in effect and discussions on the topic of whether or not the VAT should be introduced seem practically endless (e.g., Slemrod, and Bakija, 1996, pp. 209–215).

In the countries of Western Europe, the VAT was introduced after quite a long period when market traditions had finally been established. For example, in the United Kingdom and other European countries, the VAT was introduced as late as 1973, although by then the country had had a centuries-old (!) tradition of market relationships. Besides, a long period had elapsed from the time when this tax was developed to the moment when it was finally recognized and established. Specifically, EU member countries introduced the VAT after about twenty years had passed since 1954 when it was invented in France.

Today, the VAT is one of the key precedent conditions for a country joining the EU (for example, in order to become an EU member state, Finland introduced the VAT as late as July 1994). The desire to become members of the EU is exactly the key motive for which why the post-Communist countries have adopted the VAT (Tanzi, ed., 1993, Ch. 9).

It must be noted that the IMF has developed an eighteen-month schedule for the VAT's adoption (Tanzi, ed., 1993, Ch. 9). For the benefit of some countries, this schedule can even be extended; for example, in Romania, two and a half years passed in order for the VAT to be established (Tanzi, ed., 1994, Ch. 6). According to the leading former specialist, Vito Tanzi, of the IMF in fiscal issues: if there is no uniform sales tax in a country, a two-year period is required for the introduction of the VAT; this period can be reduced to a year, however, if transition to the VAT is to take place from the existing sales tax (Tanzi, 1992, p. 49). If you add to this a period of five to ten years, which, according to the IMF experts, is necessary for ensuring computer and telecommunications support of the VAT administration (IMF, 1991, Ch. V.4), there will be no doubt how long and difficult the process of introducing and establishing the VAT can be.

To this extent, one has to admit that it was a big mistake on the part of the Georgian government to make an overnight shift from a Communist-style turnover tax to the VAT. By doing this, it disregarded the first principle of the ideal taxation system previously described: simplicity. As a result, Georgia lost huge tax revenues, the public got a very negative attitude toward the VAT, and favorable conditions for the booming of corruption were created.

The IMF's mistake was that, unlike the Georgian government, it knew what negative consequences could come up after instituting the VAT. Therefore, the right action on its part would have been to recommend the

Georgian government to adopt the sales tax on a temporary basis and, in parallel, to take preparatory steps to ensure a smooth transition to the VAT. The IMF never did that. Whether or not our remark is correct can be verified by the Tax Policy Guidelines, developed by the IMF experts primarily for the benefit of economists working with the IMF missions in which it is clearly and directly stated that the introduction of the VAT should be preceded by broad taxpayer education and tax officer training campaigns. It is for this reason that, in some cases, the Fund recommends certain steps should be taken to improve sales tax collection practices before the VAT is introduced (Shome, ed., 1995, p. 280). Unfortunately, the IMF gave no such recommendation to the Georgian government.

As far as the VAT is concerned, a bigger mistake was that it was imposed on agricultural produce as well, although there had been no objective conditions for administering this tax in rural areas.

There is an assumption that has been shared by everyone in the IMF that, as a general rule, agricultural sectors of the countries in a post-Communist transformation are represented mainly by the big government-owned and cooperative companies, which can be made accountable to the VAT, and in relation to which appropriate VAT collecting practices could be developed. Small farmer businesses are exempt from the VAT, and they are responsible for paying it only in the case that their annual turnovers reach a certain upper limit (Tanzi, ed., 1993, Ch. 9). It was due to this general assumption that the Georgian government, at the IMF's insistence, imposed the VAT on agricultural production. Originally, the upper limit of annual turnover, above which all agricultural businesses should be liable for the VAT, was set at $2,300; later it was raised, first to $10,000, then up to $17,500. Finally, however, it was lowered to $12,000, which became applicable to all sectors of the economy.

Here, we have to stress the fact that, as is stated in the aforementioned Guidelines, the Fund usually identifies those sectors in which, because of certain difficulties connected with the VAT administration, it should not be applied. For example, it is recognized that agriculture should not be subject to the VAT. However, as a matter of fact, the IMF restrained itself from applying this general rule to the post-Communist countries, and the reason for doing this was because those countries had preserved large agricultural enterprises (Shome, ed., 1995, p. 280).

While applying this scheme to Georgia, the IMF failed to take into account the fact that, almost immediately after the re-establishment of national independence, all big agricultural enterprises (both government-owned and cooperative enterprises) had broken up and that by the time of making that recommendation, the Georgian agricultural sector had been represented mainly by small farmer businesses (e.g., Bezemer and Davis, 2003; Burkadze, 2007). Naturally, under such circumstances, the whole sector had been left without indirect taxation and a strong disincentive discouraged the enlargement of agricultural companies. Therefore, the growth of economic efficiency of agriculture had come up. From the perspective of the ideal taxation system, both the first principle (simplicity) and the fourth one (universality) were broken.

The Georgian government's suggestion about a potential replacement of the VAT with an increased land tax (administration of which is obviously simpler and which is practically safe from corrupted practices) was completely rejected by the IMF experts. As they explained, the reasons for their negative attitude toward this question were twofold: first, all sectors should have been subject to the VAT, as this tax had been the most developed among all other indirect taxes (IBRD, 1991, p. 31); second, the IMF experts recognized that in cases of raising the land tax rate by the level of the VAT rate, they would have been unable to develop a mechanism of recalculating it at the later stages of VAT having been paid by producers at preceding stages.

Another methodical mistake of the IMF existed in its recommendation, which later became its requirement, that the Georgian government lift the exemptions from profit tax from such parts of corporate profits that should have been used for reinvestments. By doing this, the Georgian businesses that had actually suffered from a big deficit of investments, would face a problem of losing all incentives to save some funds for business development. To do justice, one has to note that in 1995, when the IMF demanded that the said exemption be abolished because of the significant drop of production output over the preceding period, the factual extent of its applicability was very little. However, the very fact of abolishing this exemption had "washed away" from entrepreneurs' horizons, even distant hopes for getting financial incentives from the government to use their own funds for reinvestments. What should also be underlined in this respect is that, by exempting the reinvested sections of profits from any taxes (inclusive of the VAT), one may contribute to the smoothing of the profit accounting system too, ultimately possibly resulting in the growth of tax revenues. Unfortunately, the abolition of the said exemption caused negative effects to the tax accounting system in general. It should be mentioned, that according to the expert of the IMF, Krister Andersson, one of the most important steps toward improving the efficiency of tax policy is to extend investment credits (Tanzi, ed., 1993, Ch. 5).

Also evident is the IMF's mistake with respect to the progressive nature of the income tax. To shed light on this problem we must bear in mind that, under the Communist rule, all employees used to work for state-owned companies and agencies; accordingly, only staff salaries could be subject to the income tax. Under such circumstances, instead of charging tax on each individual separately, it would suffice to withhold the income tax from a company's payroll. Under the market economy, however, where, on one hand, people are involved not only in the public sector but also (and even to a greater extent) in the private sector, and on the other hand, where, in addition to salaries, they get additional income as well, such as interest, rent, dividends, and so on, the government has to deal with a problem of taxing the incomes of each individual separately.

The administering of the progressive tax requires quite a sophisticated mechanism that should be based on a taxable earnings declaration scheme. Under this scheme every individual, at the end of each calendar year, should sum up his or her earnings for the year from all sources and, accordingly, earned taxable income; after that, on the basis of a progressive schedule, he or she should calculate the taxable amount and pay it. To the extent that tax payment practices among the population are either completely nonexistent or, at best, very poorly developed, it is no surprise that very few follow such a procedure. In addition, even tax offices are not prepared to carry it out properly. For this reason, the progressive income tax only serves to facilitate the growth of a tax-evader mentality in each taxpayer and prompts him or her to break the tax law. Thus, in this case, out of the above six principles of an ideal taxation system, the first two were disregarded: *simplicity and plainness.*

From the perspective of administration, simpler by far and, accordingly, a flat income tax scheme is more transparent whereby all individual earnings are charged a uniform tax rate and nobody has to make any additional recalculations (Hall and Rabushka, 1995).

Given all that was stated above, it must be clear what a big mistake the IMF in Georgia made when it demanded an establishment of the progressive income tax scheme. The reason for the IMF's behavior seems especially obscure in the context of what their experts say in this regard. For example, Ved P. Gandhi and Dubravko Mihaljek believe that it is more reasonable to apply a flat income tax scheme in the initial phase (Tanzi, ed., 1993, Ch. 7). Leif Muten, in turn, points out that the progressive income tax scheme may create disincentives to work, and risk and discourage people from observing the tax law (Tanzi, ed., 1993, Ch. 8).

2.3.3. Mistake Resulting From Confusion

In 1995–96, the government would almost permanently raise the question of excise stamps. The IMF's position would remain categorically negative, as the IMF experts believed that the government would not be able to avoid the forgery of those marks. In 1998, however, the IMF started insisting on the opposite: it demanded, in a most categorical manner, that the government institute excise stamps on cigarettes and alcoholic beverages. In 1999, after the introduction of these excise marks, the average monthly revenues from imported cigarettes grew by 3.2 times and from locally produced cigarettes by 19.2 times. This enabled us to conclude that, over the preceding years, the country's budget must have lost huge amounts of income.

2.3.4. Mistake Resulting From a Stereotyped Approach

One of the most manifested mistakes of the IMF resulting from its stereotyped approach is the Tax Code of Georgia that was drafted by the MoF under pressure of the IMF experts and which was adopted by Parliament in late 1997. Of course, the very fact of adopting a new tax law can only be welcomed. However, the Code was written in such awkward language (perhaps because of the stereotyped translation of an English sample) that it was hardly comprehensible at time, not only to the average taxpayer, but also to specialists. In addition, some procedures described in the Code were so sophisticated that businesspeople would rather pay bribes to avoid certain confusions. It is worth noting that even the IMF had recognized that one of the reasons for inadequate tax collections may have been that the procedures were too complicated (IMF, 1997).

If we approach the Georgia Tax Code from the perspective of the previously described ideal taxation system, we can easily notice that it has altogether failed to meet all of its six principles. Furthermore, the most disappointing thing, in our opinion, is that the Code disregards the most important of those principles: simplicity.

Many government officials, researchers, businesspeople, and media people considered that one of the key reasons for the burst of the "budgetary crisis" in Georgia in 1998 was the Tax Code that contained numerous mistakes and obscurities and, therefore, was hardly understandable.

Despite the repeated attempts of some Georgian governmental officials to persuade the IMF to allow the government to reconsider the existing Tax

Code, the Fund's stance has been unchangeable: *institutional patriotism* prevents its experts from admitting their own mistakes.

2.3.5. Tactical Mistake

The adverse impact of Russia's financial crisis of August 1998—which the IMF had failed to predict (Zevin, 2001, pp. 17–18)—was first felt by Georgia as early as the beginning of September (Kakulia, 2008a, pp. 183–184). A sensitive shortage of US dollars in the Russian domestic market caused a dramatic increase for the need of US dollars in the Commonwealth of Independent States (CIS) countries. Especially sensitive to such a need were those countries for which Russia has been the most important trade partner.

In the Georgian context, the situation was aggravated by the fact that the Russian military bases existing in the Georgian territory were used as a facility for uncontrolled imports into the country of devalued Russian ruble bills with the purpose of buying and carrying US dollars to Russia. In the meantime, the Tskhinvali corridor (in South Ossetia) that had practically been beyond the Georgian government's control, was used for the intensification of smuggling cheap Russian goods and for carrying huge amounts of US dollars out of the country and into Russia. This negatively affected the exchange rate of the national currency (the lari) that had been adjusted by the NBG via implementing dollar interventions in the interbank currency exchange. Under such circumstances, the NBG had no choice but to release the dollar stocks it had kept so strictly by then. Obviously, this could not last for a long time, as the amount of such stocks was limited and could be exhausted shortly.

Under such circumstances, the IMF's recommendation was that the NGB stop implementing currency interventions and give up lari exchange rate adjustments, enabling it to preserve the NBG dollar stocks. Had the government followed this recommendation, it would inevitably have done irremediable harm to the country: the released exchange rate would have dropped immediately, provoking panic at the currency market that, in turn, would have contributed to a further decrease in the lari exchange rate. Such circumstances would have prompted people to rush to commercial banks to carry away their savings, ultimately resulting in the bankruptcy of most commercial banks and, thereafter, the impoverishment of all those individuals and companies that had kept their money with such banks.

One has to admit that the reaction of both the NBG and the government to the situation was highly commendable. They never agreed to the above advice (obviously wrong in terms of tactics) from the IMF, and had alerted commercial banks and the general public to the need of converting their lari stocks into dollars by manipulating the lari exchange rate through a gradual devaluation. Although this maneuver cost the NBG tens of millions of dollars, by the time it stopped its currency interventions into the currency market, the lari exchange rate had been as low as necessary to prevent the immediate and harmful devaluation of the Georgian currency in commercial banks (because they had already disposed of most of their lari reserves). The immediate effect of such tactical steps was that, irrespective of the destructive impact associated with the Russian financial crisis, no single commercial bank of Georgia went bankrupt for the reasons described above.

Unfortunately, the IMF experts disregarded such a generally successful performance of the Georgian government, having focused their attention on the fact that the NBG had spent a considerable part of its currency reserves.

2.3.6. Mistakes Resulting from the Abuse of Powers

The functions of the IMF and the World Bank had been delineated from each other. The IMF had repeatedly confirmed that there were certain areas, such as reformation of government-owned enterprises and public service, ensuring the right to ownership, ensuring that agreements be observed and public procurements be implemented, and so forth, with respect to which the Fund must be guided by more competent institutions and, basically, by the World Bank (IMF, 1997).

From this perspective, the IMF's categorical statement made in September 1999 seems very strange, stating that in the very near future the Georgian government would have to establish a new governmental institution: an independent, anti-corruption service endowed with broad responsibilities.

Meanwhile, a memorandum of the IMF Executive Board says that all issues related to governance, inclusive of corruption, should be considered by the Fund exclusively from an economic standpoint and within the limits of the IMF's mandate (IMF, 1997).

The fact is that in this particular case, the IMF obviously abused its powers. Only after the World Bank (having been based on both international experience and institutional underdevelopment of Georgia) had stepped in and had expressed its disagreement to the establishment of an independent anti-corruption department, the IMF "softened" its tone and shifted its focus to the possibility of applying predominantly economic mechanisms of struggle against the corrupt practices that existed in the financial system.

Another mistake related to the IMF's abuse of powers was made in the fall of 2000 when the IMF insisted that the government commit itself to raising an electricity tariff in order to address the problem of outstanding debts from the energy sector.

Meanwhile, in 1997, under the pressure of the World Bank and with the support of the IMF, Georgia established and has since operated a National Energy Regulating Committee (NERC) that was designed to be a self-governing agency, totally independent from the government. One of the key functions of the NERC was to pursue an independent tariff policy for the energy sector and to harmonize its decisions with only the principles of the market economy. Accordingly, the government had no right (and, of course, the IMF was aware of this fact) to commit itself to affecting any changes to the existing electricity tariffs. Unfortunately, the independent (from the government)—by virtue of law—NERC actually became dependent on the will of the government and, ultimately, of the IMF.

2.4. No Alternative

Despite the above mentioned criticism, the IMF had no alternative, and the existing global financial order required that Georgia performed the role of recipient country defined by that order.

Without the financial and political assistance of the West, it was practically impossible for Georgia to preserve its national independence, especially bearing in mind the hardships of economic transition and temporarily lost territories.

Irrespective of failures as described above, the IMF remained a reliable financial guarantor and a real supporter of the Georgian government in its striving to establish a sound and healthy financial and economic system for Georgia.

Indeed, the IMF was and is a strategic partner of Georgia, and it has to remain as such even after Georgia overcomes its position as a recipient country. This is true because there is no alternative for Georgia other than to become an integrated part of the civilized world.

Chapter 3

The Pre-Revolutionary State of Georgia's Economy

3.1. Balcerowicz's "Twin Brothers" in Georgia

After the presidential elections of 2000, the top leadership of the Georgian government decided to ask the US government to provide funds for financing Leszek Balcerowicz's working in Georgia as an economic adviser to the Georgian president (Papava, 2002a). The US government accepted the request.

It must be emphasized that, so far, all recommendations given by Professor Balcerowicz to the Georgian president have been strictly confidential and hidden not only from the public, but from the ministers (?!) as well it seems.

The Polish professor visits Tbilisi once in a quarter at best, and this is no wonder: shortly after he was approved as official adviser to the Georgian president, he was appointed as president of the central bank in his home country. Aside from him doing justice, we must admit that there was no real need for his more frequent visits, as he practically kept a permanent team of highly qualified experts who could keep him informed about current developments in Georgia. Furthermore, what really matters is that there was nothing extraordinarily wrong with the Georgian economy.

Below are some of the recommendations, which have become known to the public, of Professor Balcerowicz and his team:

1. The Georgian leadership should have determined very quickly what kind of economic system it was intending to build and then make the right choices. Regrettably, there was nobody among the hosts who

(perhaps because of the lack of elementary knowledge) would be able to inform him that such a choice had been made by the Georgian people by adopting the Constitution of 1995 five years earlier (which provides for the foundations of the Georgian economic system) and then by voting in 1995 and 2000 for the presidency of Eduard Shevardnadze, if we assume that the people had expressed their support (even if not always conscious one) not only to Shevardnadze personally, but also to his electoral programs that had made plenty of room for economic matters. True, if the Georgian government officers were not familiar with the president's electoral programs, why should foreign experts be expected to be so?

2. The lack of coordination within the Georgian government caused obvious dissatisfaction of the Balcerowicz team. In the context of the Georgian Constitution and the Law on the Structure and Operational Procedures of the Executive Branch of Government (which clearly vests such functions in the State Minister), such a problem should not have also been overlooked by the Georgian professionals, and they actually never did. So, why was it so necessary to waste the precious time of foreign experts, if all they could do was "discover" already obvious problems?
3. One of the most famous recommendations of Professor Balcerowicz and his Tbilisi-based team consisted of replacing the progressive system of income tax (which means that in line with the growth of personal incomes of individuals, growing 12, 15, 17 and 20 percent tax rates should be applied) with a flat system (a uniform 15-percent tax rate should be imposed) that would drastically simplify tax administration and, equally important, practically eliminate taxpayers' desire to hide incomes. In early 1992, exactly the same recommendation to the Georgian government was presented. Later, this issue was raised to the IMF on several occasions (Papava, 2002a, 2003a) but always in vain. Of course, we must welcome advice from the Polish economists. Obviously, the sensible advice of Polish experts was overlooked, and instead all of their efforts were wasted for preserving the wrong income tax policy from its further deterioration.
4. In February 2000, the president of Georgia issued a decree by which the shares in the companies, in which the government owned at least 51 percent of shares, were to be taken away from the Ministry of State Property Management and given to pertaining line ministries.

Naturally, the Balcerowicz team demanded the revocation of that clearly Communist-style decree which, above all, might invoke a conflict of interests. It is noteworthy that the decree was sharply criticized by some Georgian economists at the time when it was still under consideration. However, our criticism was not shared by the Government.

5. One of the most progressive suggestions of the Balcerowicz team concerns the pension system. As they have rightly pointed out, Georgia lacks such a system and a pension has never played the role of a pension, as such. Given the severe financial constraints of the Georgian government, the team recommended that the accent be put on private pension schemes, whereas the government should focus on paying out old debts to the people (which by that time, in total, had exceeded $150 million) and a timely performance on current obligations. The government's attitude (supported by the World Bank and which seems to be the Government's priority) consists in the reformation of the existing state pension scheme, along with creating private ones. Under the conditions of huge debts to the population, it would be a pure waste of time and effort to provide for the reformation of the state pension system. Furthermore, it would be a big mistake to suspend the process of creating private pension schemes because of that notorious state pension system.

The list of overlooked recommendations of Professor Balcerowicz and his Tbilisi-based team would presumably be much longer if they had been made available to the Georgian public. (Who knows, maybe one of the reasons for keeping them confidential was to hide the obvious weaknesses of the Georgian government team from the public.)

It is easy to notice that the poor economic policy of the Georgian government rests on the backs of Balcerowicz's "twin brothers": pressure from social and political groups, and ignorance. Moreover, those twins have never acted independently; instead, they always strengthen each other (Papava, 2002a, pp. 25).

3.2. Economic Background of the "Rose Revolution"

The fall of 2003 appeared to be a turning point in the history of independent Georgia; over the course of two days, November 22 to 23, Georgia witnessed the "Rose Revolution" (e.g., Ascherson, 2004; Baran, 2004; Radon and Onoprishvili, 2003; Welt, 2004; Zhvania, 2004). There were a number of negative factors, including economic ones that had very harmful social consequences and contributed to make this event happen.

To describe the overall economic situation in pre-revolutionary Georgia, it is important to note that the monetary system was the only sphere where macroeconomic indicators pointed to any degree of stability (Beridze and Papava, 2003; Mekantsishvili, 2009). Over the last couple of years, as a result of the NBG's restrictive monetary policy, the exchange rate of the Georgian national currency (the *lari*) remained stable and the inflation rate was fairly moderate (e.g., Chocheli and Papava, 2005; Kakulia 2001; Kakulia and Gigineishvili, 2005; Papava and Chocheli, 2003, pp. 10–17). The only significant devaluation of the lari (by 70 percent) took place in late 1998, and that devaluation was not due to internal, but to external factors (i.e., the Russian default in August 1998). As to the inflation rate, for the whole period from 1996 onward, it was slightly higher than 11 percent during only 1998–1999 (yet another negative effect of the aforementioned Russian default), whereas in all other years since 1996, it has never exceeded 7 percent a year (see Table 3.1).

Table 3.1. Annual Growth of GDP and Inflation Rate in Georgia, 1995–2003 (in percent)

	1995	1996	1997	1998	1999	2000	2001	2002	2003
Annual growth rate of GDP	3.1	10.5	11.2	2.9	3.0	1.8	4.8	5.5	11.1
Consumer price index (December over December of the previous year)	57.4	13.8	7.3	10.7	10.9	4.6	3.4	5.4	7.0

For comparison, it must be noted that in 1993–1994 the inflation rate reached 50–70 percent a month; in 1995, however, the situation started changing and the rate dropped to 57 percent a year (Gurgenidze, Lobzhanidze and Onoprishvili, 1994; Papava, 1996a, 1996b, 1999; Wang, 1998; Wellisz, 1996).

In addition to the relative stability of the monetary system, another positive trend could be observed over the recent years, namely that of consistent economic growth. In contrast to an almost threefold economic decline in 1989–1994, the highest Gross Domestic Product (GDP) growth rate was reached in 1996–1997 (11.2 percent and 10.5 percent respectively) (e.g., Papava, 1998). Although the GDP growth rate was relatively modest in 1998–2000 (3.1 percent, 2.9 percent and 1.8 percent respectively), it grew again in 2001–2002 (to 4.8 percent and 5.5 percent).

A special emphasis should be placed on the year 2003 when, because of the commencement of the Baku-Tbilisi-Ceyhan oil pipeline, the GDP growth rate reached the considerable level of 11.1 percent. It must also be noted that growth in almost all sectors of the Georgian economy was conditioned by shadow activities (Beridze, 2005). During 2003, for example, the share of the *untaxed economy* in Georgia's GDP reached 65–70 percent (e.g., Chocheli, 2003).

It is important to note that GDP growth for the first half of 2003, compared to the analogous period of 2002, also made up 9.5 percent. In other words, in the first half of 2003, GDP growth equaled the growth rate of the entire previous year, suggesting that the "Rose Revolution" had no impact from economic growth (Papava, 2005a).

Also, the so-called inflationary component of the "Rose Revolution" was not as serious as it could have been (Papava, 2005a). According to the Indicative Plan of Georgia's Economic and Social Development (IPGESD) for 2003, the annual inflation rate was expected to be around 5–7 percent, whereas from January to October 2003, the actual rate was very low at 1.9 percent. In November, during the period of one month, under the conditions of a revolutionary situation, the inflation rate grew to 4.8 percent. This was a direct result not only of the political instability, but also of provocative statements made by government officials about the diminished supply in the Georgian market and the inevitable growth in prices of consumer goods because of the approaching revolution. No doubt, such statements intensified people's anticipation of inflation.

Even in spite of these statements and the volatile political situation, the actual inflation rate for 2003 was never higher than 7 percent (i.e., it never exceeded the expected upper threshold projected in the 2003 IPGESD). This was largely because the new post-revolutionary government, under the leadership of Mr. Mikheil Saakashvili, had the full confidence of the Georgian people and because the NGB continued to pursue its tight monetary policy (Kakulia and Gigineishvili, 2005).

To sum up what was stated above about the inflationary component of the "Rose Revolution", the revolution actually managed, in a sense, to squeeze itself into the projected limits of the inflation rate and, therefore, the "Rose Revolution" did not "cost" the Georgian people too much.

Now the question that arises is this: If the economic growth rate in 2003 was satisfactory and the inflation rate was moderate, what was the macroeconomic component of the "Rose Revolution"?

3.3. The Budgetary Crisis in the Georgian Context

Many economists and politicians in Georgia believe the alleged economic crisis (e.g., Gotsiridze and Kandelaki, 2001) in Georgia to be one of the key reasons of the "Rose Revolution". Although this explanation may seem quite attractive at first glance because of its simplicity, it does not accurately describe the pre-revolutionary situation in Georgia's economy.

Indeed, the fact that there was no economic crisis before the "Rose Revolution" would look quite logical if one recalls that economic theory knows just two types of economic crises: those of *overproduction* and those of *underproduction*.

As we know, when a crisis is due to overproduction, supply by far exceeds demand and the amount of unsold products keeps mounting, whereas prices are drastically dropping. As a result, companies go out of business one after another and the unemployment rate keeps growing.

As to the crisis of underproduction, demand is much larger than supply in this case, as a result of which prices go up, stimulating the growth of supply in the long run.

As was noted above, recent years saw relatively stable economic growth and moderate inflation, which are clear indications that there were no symptoms of an economic crisis in Georgia for whatever cause, either overproduction or underproduction.

In order to properly understand the macroeconomic preconditions of the "Rose Revolution", it is necessary to draw attention to the country's budgetary problems. Specifically, focus should be placed on the year 1998, marked by both a devaluation of the national currency (which, as was noted earlier, was an immediate effect of the Russian default in August 1998) and the emergence of major gaps in the national budget that ultimately led to actual revenues considerably below projected ones. The starkest example of this phenomenon was the year 1999 when the budget deficit reached $150 million, or about 30 percent of the projected total tax revenues.

I believe that *budgetary crisis* would be the most accurate description of this long, drawn-out process that stretched into late 2003. Specific elements of the government's overall failure to fully collect projected revenues were:

1. Failure to fully collect projected tax revenues;
2. Failure to fully collect projected non-tax revenues such as those resulting from the privatization of state-owned property;
3. Failure to receive all available loans and grants from international financial institutions and donor countries.

Each of the elements had a number of specific causes. With that in mind, it must be stressed that the first of those elements (i.e., the failure to collect projected tax revenues in full) had an immense influence on the two other.

As described above, in practically all years since 1998 onward, major gaps in the national budget appeared between projected tax revenues and actual revenues. Moreover, the Tax Code of Georgia was adopted by the Georgian Parliament in late 1997, leading many politicians and economists in Georgia to quite rightly believe that the new tax legislation was the immediate cause that prompted the budgetary crisis to emerge (see Ch. 2, 2.3).

The IMF experts proposed a draft tax code to the GoG. It was based on a model tax code that IMF specialists had developed, taking into account both theory and international practice of taxation. As a matter of fact, however, the "ideal" tax law was based on the assumption that all national borders were under the control of national border and customs authorities. Yet this by no means reflected Georgian reality. Unfortunately, the territories of Abkhazia and South Ossetia, major channels of smuggled goods coming from Russia to Georgia, were then and continue to be beyond the Georgian government's control.

The government, in turn, significantly contributed toward worsening an already bad tax code. In a few years, it made thousands of amendments and additions to the tax code that ultimately led to its transformation into a totally confusing document that simply paved the way for uncurbed corruption in the taxation system.

Personal interests of corrupted government officials and numerous lacunae in the tax code that were quite easy to conceal made the existing gap between actual and projected tax revenues even larger.

A remarkable peculiarity of the Georgian phenomenon of the budgetary crisis was the so-called "war of budgets" that has been waged for about a decade between the national budget and that of the Autonomous Republic of Ajara. It consists of a refusal by the leadership of the autonomous republic to fill the central budget with legitimately established portions of fiscal revenues raised within their jurisdiction. According to the Ajarian leaders, the reason they refused to contribute to the national budget was that the central government was allegedly failing to provide them with funds from the national budget. Whatever the reason they were not contributing funds, the fact remains that the national budget and, ultimately, all other regions of Georgia have been short of receivable budgetary transfers. Such circumstances further aggravated the budgetary crisis that had already existed in the country.

Additionally, corrupt government officials resorted to various fraudulent machinations to achieve a fictitious implementation of the national budget revenues. These were specifically widespread, including: the practices of compelling companies to pay taxes in advance, returning collected taxes to taxpayers by means of forged documents, filing fictitious offsets, and artificially raising the prices of public procurements so that they could pocket the difference between official and actual prices.

To compensate for the gap between actual and projected tax revenues, the GoG invented fictitious increases in planned non-tax revenues of the national budget. For example, they often artificially raised the earnings from the privatization of state-owned property in the national budget revenues. In practice, however, these earnings were significantly smaller than what they were represented to be and, as a result, the actual budget fell even further behind the official projections.

The failures to receive all available loans and grants from international financial institutions and donor countries were primarily caused by the government's inability from 1999 onward to implement the IMF programs without any delay. This problem became especially painful in 2002 when the IMF suspended its programs in Georgia. Moreover, this led to the blocking of all financial assistance to Georgia from other international financial institutions and, in addition, aggravated the problem of foreign debt, which made up about 50 percent of the GDP by that time. Without debt restructuring in the Paris Club, Georgia would have been unable to manage this huge debt.

The suspension of the IMF program was an immediate result of both the government's inability to adopt and implement a realistic national budget and the deferment of almost all reforms oriented toward democratization and a free market system.

In June of 2003, Georgian President Eduard Shevardnadze issued an ordinance by which he approved the Economic Development and Poverty Reduction Program of Georgia (EDPRP) for 2003–2015 (GoG, 2003). This program was developed in close cooperation between the public authorities, and the NGOs and academic experts. At a later stage, experts from international financial institutions and donor governments joined them. Unfortunately, because of its usual lack of political will, the Shevardnadze government never even attempted to embark on the implementation of this program. Indeed, the Shevardnadze government's apathetic attitude toward the program resulted in the extreme deterioration of Georgia's relationship with the IMF and other international donors.

In 2003, as a result of the government's numerous failures in all aspects related to the budgeting process, the national budget deficit reached $90 million, i.e., 15 percent of projected budget revenues. By the end of 2003, the aggregate internal debt accumulated as the government consistently failed to pay salaries and pensions to public sector employees and pensioners. During the years of budget crisis, internal debt reached around $120 million, of which unpaid pensions totaled $70 million (even though monthly pensions in Georgia were as low as $7 per month).

Unsurprisingly, with such financial problems in place, the poverty rate in Georgia reached 52 percent at the time. Deteriorating social problems and the overall dissatisfaction with the Shevardnadze regime in Georgian society created an unsustainable budget crisis, the logical consequence of which was the "Rose Revolution".

Chapter 4

The Post-Revolutionary Development of Georgia's Economy

4.1. Starting Points for the Post-Revolutionary Government

Georgia's young (including in terms of age) and, in many respects, inexperienced government inherited numerous unsolved problems from the Shevardnadze administration; from which one should distinguish the following:

- energy crisis, which means that with the coming of winter, the whole of Georgia had to survive without electricity and heating;
- budgetary crisis, in the sense that because of the inability and unwillingness of public officers to collect taxes, the government accumulated huge arrears of pensions and salaries in the public sector.

Most of such problems were conditioned, first of all, by a high degree of corruption (Dadalauri, 2008). Therefore, the key challenge of the new post-revolution government was to combat corruption.

At the same time, the government which had come to power by means of revolution was exposed to a temptation of strengthening the vertical axis of power and minimizing elements of a decentralized system of governance, justifying it by a need to reinstate the country's territorial integrity.

From the moment of his coming to power, Mr. Saakashvili set a goal to concentrate powers in the President's hands (Khechinashvili, 2005, p.3). To this end, as early as in February 2004, a number of amendments were added to the Georgian Constitution, owing to which the President obtained the power to dismiss the government or, alternatively, to disband the parliament and order extraordinary parliamentary elections, should the parliament and the government be in conflict with each other. The natural consequence of this kind of constitutional novelty was the growth of parliament's loyalty not only to the president, but also to his government, in turn, leading to the significant weakening of parliament as a political institution.

In late 2006, under pressure from the Council of Europe, President Saakashvili proposed amendments to the Constitution that would allow for an extraordinary presidential election in case of a repeated dismissal of the parliament.

Whereas before coming to power Mr. Saakashvili and his team harshly criticized Shevardnadze for his reluctance to allow for the direct elections of mayors in the major cities, he abandoned the idea of directly elected mayors after his election.

The lack of any more or less critical remarks, with respect to the above-described presidential power reinforcing developments on the West's part, stimulated further growth of authoritarian tendencies in the public governance (see, Areshidze, 2007, pp. 197-295).

4.2. Achievements in Reforms

The strengthening of presidential powers in Georgia had some positive implications in terms of establishing a financial order in the country; accomplishing some significant increases in tax revenues; and, as a consequence, overcoming the above-mentioned budgetary crisis (see, Areshidze, 2007, pp. 191-195). As a result, the post-revolution government succeeded in paying off all accumulated debts to pensioners and public sector employees. In the summer of 2004, this all led to the IMF program's renewal that had been terminated in 2003 due to the incapability and extremely corrupted nature of the Shevardnadze administration. Consequently, Georgia managed to achieve macroeconomic stability (Cordonnier, 2008; Khaduri, 2005a).

It is important to note that, immediately after the "Rose Revolution", members of government and civil society wrongly believed that the relationship between the GoG and the Ajarian leadership could be improved and that the aforementioned war of budgets would come to end. Later developments proved that expectations of a closer cooperation were illusory and not only in the arena of budgets (Gegeshidze, 2004; Tsereteli, 2004). However, after the revolution (ICG, 2004) of May 6, 2004, in the Autonomous Republic of Ajara, new opportunities for arranging normal budgeting processes between the central government and this region of Georgia had emerged.

As far as the goal of overcoming the long, drawn-out budgetary crisis is concerned, it was particularly important to adopt a new tax code that would be based on generally accepted principles of making the tax burden lighter and the taxation system simpler (Chappell, 1990). That is what many international experts suggested immediately after the "Rose Revolution" (e.g., Phillips, 2004). Remarkably, President Saakashvili was one of the early advocates of such changes, long before the revolution. Soon after the "Rose Revolution", a special governmental commission of experts was established that started working on a draft of the new tax legislation, and the Parliament adopted that new legislation at the end of 2004 (Dadalauri, 2009; Khaduri, 2006). In the new tax code, VAT decreased from 20 percent to 18 percent, the payroll tax decreased from 32 percent to 20 percent, and a flat income tax of 12 percent replaced the old progressive income tax. Reducing the import-tax base for agricultural products and construction materials, as well as annulling the import taxes for other goods, have made Georgia much more competitive. The special reforms were implemented for strengthening the tax administration (Curnow, 2006).

Among other achievements of the Saakashvili government, one should also mention a significantly simplified licensing system for launching new businesses.

The launch of a large-scale privatization program should also be regarded as one of the key accomplishments of the post-revolution government.

The new Labor Code was revolutionary. By limiting the rights of employees, it had substantially broadened those of employers. Although this may encourage businesses to develop, it also leaves employees unprotected.

After the publication of the World Bank's rating list in 2006 entitled "Doing Business," according to which Georgia had made an impressive jump from the 112th to the 37th place among the world's nations, the Georgian Government announced that its objective would be to push the country forward and to ensure that Georgia would be found among the 20 best nations of the world in the World Bank's next year's rating list. Furthermore, it did assume the 18th place in 2007; in 2010 Georgia appeared the 12th place (WB, 2010). Surprisingly, in the ranking list of 151 countries according to the size of the shadow economy, which also was prepared by the experts of the World

Bank, Georgia was on the bottom in 2007 (Schneider, Buehn, and Montenegro, 2010, p. 29).

It is important to stress that the government should strive and provide for public wealth and prosperity and not for higher places in rating lists. As far as ratings are concerned, the government should pay more attention to the Economist Intelligence Unit Quality of Life Index (EIU, 2005) and the UNDP Human Development Index (UNDP, 2010) by which, much to the people's disadvantage, Georgia ranks 87th and 74th respectively.

Among some other accomplishments of the post-revolution government, one should emphasize the qualitative improvement of the country's criminal situation (Kupatadze, 2007).The strengthening of presidential powers enabled the government to start an effective fight against corruption. In this context, one must mention the abolition of traffic police that had existed since the Soviet times, as well as the creation of a western-style patrol police, in a very short period of time. As a consequence, the shameful practice of bribery across the country's roads and highways was exterminated.

The combat of corruption in the energy sector resulted in overcoming the energy crisis: as of the winter of 2006-2007, the whole of Georgia has been enjoying about a 100 percent supply of electricity.

Among the post-revolution government's accomplishments, one should emphasize the introduction of national examinations for admission to universities, replacing the old corrupt system of separate admission exams in individual universities that existed since the Soviet times.

A four-fold growth of the national budget revenues was achieved as a result of such anti-corruption measures as the arresting and releasing of former government officials and their relatives for a "price of liberty". Officially, this was proclaimed as paying back money and properties to the State that had been stolen from it (McDonald, 2005). Such revenues could not be raised on a regular basis. At best, they could be collected for one more time and with a much lesser effect. The government, specifically for this purpose, established extra-budgetary "law-enforcement development accounts," whereby those suspected of corrupt practices were compelled to transfer payments to buy their liberty.

The achievements in reforms have promoted the considerable increasing of Georgia's attractiveness for foreign direct investments (FDIs) (e.g., Aslamazishvili, 2005; Burduli, 2008; Shmidt, 2007).

The Armed Forces of Georgia were radically overhauled, with a defense budget fueled by revenue increases, and with assistance from the United States and other NATO member states. Military readiness improved greatly, and Georgian forces that served abroad received high marks from coalition officers.

4.3. Pseudo Reforms

Some of the Georgian government's actions defy both economic theory and common sense. Chief among these was the president's generous summer 2006 initiative to add 50,000 people to a national employment program (CG, 2006c). The idea was to require private entrepreneurs to give three-month jobs to unemployed persons. For this, the latter were to be paid $85 a month out of the national budget (Tokmazishvili and Archvadze, 2007). (In the summer of 2006, after the enactment of the new Labor Code, unemployment allowances, $12.40 per month, were abolished.) The program cost the national budget $12.7 million. In principle, no business with the demand to expand should need any direct assistance from the national budget. All the government needed to do was to provide for the development of professional training or retraining programs, and the Georgian government had rightly assumed this duty (e.g., Burduli and Arevadze, 2010; Natelauri, 2010).

This program, however, employed only a few people. In most cases, a simple deal was made. Businessmen agreed to subscribe to any contract under which they could pretend that they employed some people who did some job. Such a deal also made an unemployed person happy because he made $255 in three months for doing nothing. There were, however, rather perverted situations as well. Some businessmen agreed to subscribe to such contracts on the condition that new "employees" shared half of the sum with them.

The average share of salaries in the costs of production is typically twenty percent, and so $12.7 million spent on salaries should produce goods and services worth about $60 million. Although there were no official employment statistics under this program, we should expect that about ten percent of the targeted number of beneficiaries were actually employed. This means, then, that $12.7 million was spent out of the national budget for the production of goods and services, with an aggregate value of perhaps $6 million.

In essence, it can be said that $12.7 million allocated from the national budget was nothing but an allowance for the unemployed. This amount went to the market ostensibly with the purpose of producing consumer goods, but because no actual goods and services were produced, the only contribution was to the growth of inflation. Consequently, any measures of this kind, however generous their objectives might be, cannot, in fact, produce any desired results. On the contrary, all they can do, along with other similar measures, is to contribute to macroeconomic destabilization (CG, 2006a).

Unfortunately, the same type of national employment program covering 100,000 people was started in December 2007.

4.4. Errors and Offenses

Among the negative consequences of the strengthened presidential and weakened parliamentary powers, one should distinguish an intensified feeling of impunity among the government officers which, in the first place, has been manifested in a gross disrespect for the rule of law. Humorously, the significantly weakened parliament is often called the "Government's Notary". As to the judiciary branch, it has become an appendix to the General Prosecutor's Office and the whole executive branch (e.g., Anjaparidze, 2006a).

The government's control of media and, most of all, TV channels has become overwhelming. Some independent TV channels ("Channel 9," "Iberia," later "202") and popular newspapers ("Dilis Gazeti," "Mtavari Gazeti") were closed shortly after the "Rose Revolution". Other popular private TV stations became completely controlled by the government (CG, 2005, HRIDC, 2008a).

Redundancies in the government were combined with gross mistakes in staffing and institutional policies. In all government agencies, most experienced employees were swept away (in most cases in violation of the law). All governmental institutions were mainly staffed by the youth who had received some international training. As a consequence, the government ministries and departments were deprived of experienced staff which led to the loss of "institutional memory".

The government's mistakes in the reorganization of the ministries and departments, and the loss of "institutional memory" were supplemented with the non-professionalism of many post-revolution ministers. The most blatant example of non-professionalism was the entrustment of the Minister of Defense with a task to deal with the marketing of Georgian wines abroad in the spring of 2006. Other examples of this kind was the abolition of the State anti-monopoly service in late 2004, and Mr. Saakashvili's initiative in the fall of 2007 to empower the Ministry of the Interior (which, in Georgia, combines the police and the national security forces) to deal with the anti-monopoly regulation of the domestic market. Later, after Russian-Georgian 5-days war in

August 2008, President Saakashvili had again empowered the Ministry of the Interior, but now to deal with the contraction of the houses for IDPs.

The revolutionary wave also gave the government enough courage to re-organize some ministries and departments. In particular, the State Department of Statistics (SDS), which before the revolution had been an independent agency accountable to the president, also fell victim to revolutionary reorganizations. It was also incorporated in the Ministry of Economic Development, perhaps the most palpable example of a conflict of interests (Vaicenavičius, 2008). As a consequence, statistics play the same role in Georgia as they did in the Soviet times when they were assigned a political function to proclaim an annual improvement of the country's economic status.

One has to emphasize the corruption transformations in post-revolution Georgia. The extra-budgetary accounts, which used to accumulate incomes from accused people paying the "price of liberty", were already described above. Because such accounts were outside the budgetary area, it was natural that there was no transparency in terms of spending as well. However, the problem became even more serious as the government started replenishing those accounts by means of the so-called "voluntary contributions" of businesses (e.g., Anjaparidze, 2006b). As a result, if pre-revolutionary functionaries had pockets open for bribes, their post-revolutionary successors that had closed pockets opened bank accounts. In the beginning, the IMF turned a blind eye to the existence of such accounts due to an erroneous assumption that all means are good to fight corruption. Obviously, it had forgotten a simple truth that it is a futile endeavor to beat corruption by means of corruption. Later, in the spring of 2006, under the IMF's pressure, the "extra-budgetary" accounts were abolished.

The post-revolution government's disrespect for the Constitution and laws became evident in the privatization process of public property when by means of bypassing the law, or much rather in its complete defiance, some new owners started to "emerge" from nowhere (Gujaraidze, 2010; Gujaraidze, Barbakadze, Gujaraidze, Mchedlishvili and Kakhaberi, 2007).

The process of "de-privatization" that was launched after the "Rose Revolution" is another reason for being worried. De-privatization in the context of a post-revolutionary Georgia means that certain objects that had been privatized before the revolution were forcibly taken back by the government and later offered for privatization. Throughout the process, law-enforcement organs (the General Prosecutor's Office and the Ministry of the Interior) got involved, pressuring the owners to "voluntarily" give up their property for the government's benefit. At the same time, there was no guarantee that a need for another de-privatization would not be brought onto the agenda at sometime in the future again (Papava, 2000a, 2006b). The actual goal of the government was to redistribute property for the benefit of the newly formed elite.

One should also be worried about some other examples of the post-revolutionary government's defiance associated with property rights such as extrajudicial decisions to demolish privately owned residential houses built before the revolution, the owners of which had all relevant documents certifying both ownership and legitimacy of construction. The only argument presented by the government in justifying such demolitions was a desire to improve the city's "image." The government did not seem to be concerned at all (HRIDC, 2008b) that property rights were being grossly infringed upon (Christiansen, 2006). Paradoxically, the Georgian government's obvious disrespect for one's property rights never became subject of Western criticism. Furthermore, as it was mentioned above, in the World Bank's ranking list for Year 2007, titled Doing Business, Georgia, the country where private ownership wad not protected in any way, held the 18th place which, by itself, deserves very little confidence.

Against the background of a successful fight with mass corruption, there still remains the unsolved problem of elite corruption, involving high-level government officers who in defiance of public procurement regulations and with total impunity, have been using budgetary resources for their own benefits, and have been exploiting their official status to protect their favorite companies under their umbrella (e.g., Natelauri, 2009). The most palpable example of such a kind of corruption is the former defense minister, Irakli Okruashvili, who was charged with corruption after his switching from the government team to the vigorous opposition of President Saakashvili. The Okruashvili lesson is exemplary for the other cabinet and parliamentary majority members to the extent that now everyone will know that nobody may be "assured" against the discovery of his or her corrupt behaviors, should anybody dare to move into opposition. At the same time, the Okruashvili story is typical to the extent that it shows how "effectively" the Saakashvili administration exploited the combat of corruption against its political opponents: until Mr. Okruashvili remained to be the cabinet member, he used to be proclaimed by Saakashvili as an ideal minister and one who should be an example to others (CG, 2006b); after he left the government, the presidential team chose not to make any comments about his behavior; and only after Mr. Okruashvili publicly announced his political ambitions was he accused of corruption.

In the context of the above-described negative consequences of the post-revolutionary government's activities, they do fit quite well with multiple violations of human rights (including murders of young people by policemen for which, as broadly believed by the public, not all responsible persons received fair punishment) (Devdariani, 2004; HRIDC, 2004, 2007), which have repeatedly been incorporated in the Public Defender's reports (e.g., CG, 2008j; Subari, 2007) and seem not quite unexpected. Until recently, the West's criticism for these and many other facts was so "soft" that the Saakashvili government had no real reason to take any more-or-less effective steps to rectify existing mistakes, not to mention any preventive measures (Papava, 2009b).

4.5. The Russian Track

In post-Revolution Georgia, the so-called "Northern Way", or Georgia's integration into Russia's economic domain, had become prominent (Papava, 2006c, 2008g).

In 2003, Anatoliy Chubais, the President of the Management Board of RAO EES (Unified Energy Systems) of Russia and prominent Russian statesman and political figure, wrote that Russia should establish a "Liberal Empire" in the post-Soviet world (Chubais, 2003; Simons, 2008, pp. 70-81; Torbakov, 2003). By calling it "liberal," there was a sense that the new empire should be based on economics rather than coercion wherein Russian companies (public and private) should take over the ownership of strategic companies in the former Soviet republics which (Kissinger, 2002, p. 76), in the long run, must lead to the re-establishment of Moscow's political influence over those countries.

According to its architects, a Liberal Empire should be created not by a forced armed occupation of the former Soviet republics, but by gaining control over the main economic facilities (by means of acquiring and developing assets) located on their territory. An essentially universal analysis of Russian investments in the CIS countries is presented in an article by Crane, Peterson and Oliker (2005). It is also important to note that in the Russian idea of a "Liberal Empire," its developers and executors implied non-military methods of creation in the word "liberal," and not of the functioning (which they did not mention at all) of this "empire". This is essentially not surprising if we keep in mind the far from democratic and liberal nature of Russia (Åslund, 2005; Trenin, 2005). Herein, we should note the interrelationships of Russian policy in the post-Soviet space of energy dependence and political independence (Balzer, 2005) whereby the latter weakens when the former increases (Smith, 2004, pp. 5-8). It is no accident that, for Russia along with the formation of a Liberal Empire, a targeted advance towards creating an Energy Empire was of particular importance (Hill, 2004).

Russia started fulfilling its master plan in Armenia, its strategic partner in the region. In late 2002, on the eve of the presidential election in Armenia, a Russian-Armenian treaty called the "debt-for-equity" swap was executed (Perovič, 2005). In early 2006, Russia obtained new assets in exchange for not raising Armenia's price for natural gas. Since Russia and Armenia did not share a border, and in view of the frozen conflict between Armenia and Azerbaijan, Georgia was the lynchpin in the economic space of Russia and Armenia. If Georgia was dragged into the Liberal Empire, the fate of Azerbaijan would have be determined as well, given the fact that all of its strategic economic projects were linked with Georgia (Papava, 2006a, 2008e).

The first step towards snaring Georgia in the liberal empire's net was the summer of 2003 takeover of the shares of a US-based company, the AES Silk Road by RAO EES (Gularidze, 2003).

The involvement of Russian energy companies into the Georgian economy was in progress after the Russian-Georgian war in August 2008. In 2011 the Government sold the hydro power plants, Khrami 1 and Khrami 2, to INTER RAO, the Russian company established in 2008 after the reorganization and disintegration of the RAO EES into several companies (Chubais, 2008), for $104 million. It is noteworthy that Khrami 1 and Khrami 2 were under the management of INTER RAO, based on the Agreement with RAO EES concluded in 2000. The Agreement was concluded for 25 years, expiring as of 2024. According to a statement by the government, INTER RAO had also undertaken the responsibility, by the Agreement, to build three new hydro power plants for which the investment of $193 million was to be made (Patsuria, 2011).

The Georgian government fully supported the entry of the Russian investments into the Georgian economy during the large-scale privatization of government-owned enterprises after the "Rose Revolution". The best example was the sale of Georgian gold and copper mining and processing companies to Stanton Equities, a subsidiary of the Russian holding group, Industrial Investors.

Encouraged by the government's affinity for Russian investments, the owners of the United Georgian Bank (privatized in 1995) sold it to Russia's Vneshtorgbank, of which 99-percent is owned by the Russian government.

This sale was the nationalization of the United Georgian Bank by the Russian government. This takeover came on the tails of Vneshtorgbank's acquisition of Armenia's Armsberbank (Liloyan, 2004).

Gazprom was especially aggressive. It has made several attempts to take over the gas pipeline that connects Armenia with Russia. In late 2005 and early 2006, the Georgian government negotiated with Gazprom, ostensibly to sell the gas pipeline. It is not clear, however, why selling the pipeline to the Russian government-owned gas company should be considered as "privatization." After America's intervention, the Georgian government's talks with Gazprom came to an end (MCC, 2005), giving a heavy blow to Russia's plans.

In late 2006, in the context of doubling the price for Russian gas, Gazprom tried to take over some of Georgia's energy assets once again (Socor, 2006). The same problem existed with the Georgian Railway, the purchasing of which was under the interests of the Russian state-run railway operator (CG, 2008i).

Regrettably, it is evident that Georgia is being culled into Russia's "liberal empire" (Papava, 2010c; Papava, and Starr, 2006).

After the "Rose Revolution", the Kazakh capital invasion of the Georgian economy was also remarkable (Salieva, and Matayev, 2007). The entry of the Kazakh government-owned companies into the Georgian market was, for some reason, labeled as "privatization" (probably in order to create a reform image for the government).

Does anything with origins in the West—in Europe—take root in the Georgian economy? The purchase of the Bank Republic by the French Société Générale, for example, or the Bank of Georgia's offering at the London Stock Exchange show this to be true, but these examples are exceptions rather than the rule.

4.6. THE ROLE OF THE WEST

While the post-revolutionary government achievements were enthusiastically commended by the leaders of the Western nations and various international organizations, the mistakes (as were repeatedly noted above) were unfortunately subject to, at best, moderate criticism. Naturally, the question arose: Why did the West choose to turn a blind eye to such mistakes, and why was it only after November 7, 2007 that an avalanche of criticism dropped upon Mikheil Saakashvili along with his government and the parliamentary majority?

The West's captivation of Mr. Saakashvili resulted from, first of all, the fact that he was perceived by all as example of a successful post-Soviet leader with a Western university education from the very beginning. Furthermore, by his numerous passionate speeches and interviews, especially in the West, he managed to procure the image of an advocate of Western democratic values, human rights and a market economy. It is important to note that, unlike his speeches made for the West, his public appearances in Georgia, especially after his coming to power, were clearly and predominantly aggressive with respect to the people of his country (the most typical example of his aggressive speeches is one that he made in one of his public appearances before the Georgian TV channels when he called the senior generation of the Georgian scholars and public figures as the people who must be "flushed down"). This kind of aggression, combined with the above-described negative consequences of the Saakashvili administration, contributed to the gradual development among experts to form the opinion that Georgia had been ruled by an authoritative regime and that embryonic democratic elements of governance had been getting weaker every day (e.g., Lazarus, 2010; Mitchell, 2007; Walker, 2007).

Official statements of the Georgian leadership regarding Georgia's desire to join NATO and EU, Georgian military groups' participation in the antiterrorist coalition in Iraq, and peacekeeping forces in Kosovo and Afghanistan were considered as a proof of the post-revolutionary government's pro-Western orientation. To do justice, it must be noted that similar statements had been made before the "Rose Revolution", and the first military missions to Kosovo and Iraq had also been sent out before the revolution.

The West also liked (especially before the Russian-Georgian war in August 2008) President Saakashvili's clearly anti-Russian rhetoric which, most of all, had been manifested in tough (sometimes even cynical) criticism of Russia's top political leadership (e.g., Kakachia, 2010; Khelashvili, 2011). Very little attention was attached to the fact that Georgia widely "opened the doors" for Russian investments after the "Rose Revolution", and these interests have, by no means, diminished despite that Russia declared the closing of its market for Georgian agricultural products from the spring of 2006 (e.g., Anjaparidze, 2006c, Gaganidze, 2007; Parsons, 2006, Tsereteli, 2006; Uzagalieva, 2007; Vincentz, 2006). At the same time, the Kremlin's unhidden and intense dislike for Georgia's post-revolutionary government

(Papava, 2007b) and its personal dislike of President Saakashvili (at times, combined with open aggression against Georgia, and the annexation of the Georgian provinces of Abkhazia and South Ossetia) contributed to the further growth of the West's support of Georgia and its leadership which had been pretty extensive even before the "Rose Revolution".

Georgia's pro-Western and anti-Russian course was exactly the reason why the West turned a blind eye to the above-described negative consequences of the post-revolutionary government's activities. Apparently, the government was the first to realize this. Especially after President George W. Bush's visit to Georgia in May 2005, the Georgian leadership's behavior started showing the symptoms of a certain "forgiven-for-all syndrome", and it was believed that the visit of the American president to Georgia was an adequate indulgence and exoneration by the West for any anti-democratic actions of the post-revolutionary government, not only for already committed ones but also for those which might be committed in the future.

Georgia's experience teaches that a pro-Western and an anti-Russian orientation are by no means a firm and adequate guarantee of democracy (Cecire, 2011; Papava, 2008c).

4.7. Economic Constituent of the 2008 Presidential and Parliamentary Elections

In November 2007, to rescue his own image as well as that of Georgia, President Saakashvili resigned and called for an extraordinary presidential election for January 5, 2008. On May 21, 2008, a parliamentary election was carried out. During both campaigns, it was apparent that Mr. Saakashvili and his party were using administrative resources for their own interests. The elections were competitive, considering the circumstances, and polling was mostly uneventful. In the final accounting, Mr. Saakashvili received slightly more than the fifty percent required to avert a run-off, whilst the "National Movement" now controls 80 percent of the seats in Parliament. International observers gave qualified approval to the campaign environment and election conduct, but they also have mentioned serious reservations about using administrative resources, and the transparency and fairness of the ballot counting (OSCE, 2008a, 2008b).

During both of the pre-election campaigns, a stake was made on the social problems, especially on overcoming the poverty in the country. Mikheil

Saakashvili and his political party declared, as their pre-election slogan, achievement of the following goal: "Unified Georgia without Poverty!" It is worth mentioning that the social issues prevailed in the pre-election campaigns of the opposition leaders in the Presidential elections and in those of the parties in the Parliamentary elections.

Having won both of the elections, the government embarked on fulfilling the responsibilities taken before the voters. For this purpose, the basic provisions of the five-year poverty eradication program were published. The program mentions reducing the poverty by half rather than fully eradicating poverty (e.g., CG, 2008d). For the sake of justice, it should be emphasized that the relative poverty cannot actually be eradicated because as the level of the economic development increases the poverty line also increases, below which there is always a certain segment of the population. By avoiding the concept of the poverty line in its program, the government did not undertake the responsibility to eradicate the poverty which used to be a key slogan of President Saakashvili and his political party in the pre-election races.

Within the framework of the five-year governmental program, the government's 50-Day Action Plan was worked out (CG, 2008f, 2008k), scheduled for implementation within the first five months of 2008; that is, from January to May, for a total of 152 days. Some projects included in the Plan were directed towards economic development and, consequently, reducing the level of poverty whilst some other projects are questionable from the economic point of view.

Within the framework of the government's 50-Day Action Plan, a so-called "revolutionary" economic package of laws was developed (CG, 2008e) with the main goal of turning Georgia into a global financial center by offering tax exemptions on income to large financial companies whose activity in Georgia did not exceed ten percent of their financial turnover. This "revolutionary" package also provided for a significant reorganization of the NBG, the country's central bank, by aiming at actually subordinating it to the government as exceeding the threshold level of annual inflation, allowed the government to put forward the issue of resigning the president of the NBG to Parliament (CG, 2008a).

Among the projects that stimulated economic development, the creation of financing, in the form of so-called "cheap credits" for small business development, needs to be highlighted (Abesadze and Kakulia, 2009). Unfortunately, this attractive project for many beginner businessmen was carried out without sufficient transparency and, most surprisingly, the decisions about the issuing of these credits for each concrete project were taken not by a credit institution hired by the government for this purpose, but by the government itself at its meetings.

The government's 50-Day Action Plan includes the responsibility of increasing pensions, which was one of the promises made during the Presidential and Parliamentary elections, with the amount of a monthly pension increasing by 27 percent in April. Another promise was increasing the minimum pension up to $100 in 2009 which, considering the current exchange rate, implies an increase of more than two times.

The following two projects, the opening of a free economic zone (FEZ) in the proximity of the port city of Poti and the emission of Eurobonds, are also to be highlighted from among the doubtful projects envisaged by the government's 50-Day Action Plan.

The problem of opening a FEZ in Georgia was not a new one and was an idea which was, first of all, linked with the province of Ajara when its former leader, Aslan Abashidze, raised the issue of creating such a zone near another port city of Batumi fifteen years before the "Rose Revolution" (e.g., Khutsidze, 2003). Considering that Georgia embarked on liberalizing its foreign trade more than ten years ago, when business registration procedures had also been liberalized during the post-revolutionary period, the economic viability of setting up the FEZ is doubtful to a greater extent (Papava, 2007c). Apart from this, it is necessary to take into account the international experience of setting up a FEZ in countries with a lack of investment or with an "investment hunger" which ends up in increased "hunger" as the investors (both the foreign and domestic) prefer to run their businesses within the zone (mainly because of the tax exemptions) and not outside the zone, as a result of which the economy mostly develops within the zone and not beyond its borders. Thus, the economic development of the country outside the FEZ is hampered due to the existence of the latter. Unfortunately, this danger is very real in the case of the Georgian economy (Patsuria, 2008). Regretfully, these arguments against establishing the FEZ (Khutsidze, 2007) were not shared by the Government that signed an agreement of Investment Authority for the UAE's Ras Khaimah, as with the development company in this zone near Poti. It is equally important to mention that this Arab company also purchased 51 percent of the shares of the same Poti sea port (CG, 2008g).

The second suspicious project within the framework of the government's 50-Day Action Plan was the issuance of $500 million worth of Eurobonds with a maturity of five years and with a coupon set at 7.5 percent in April 2008 (CG, 2008b, 2008c). In 2013, Georgia will have to cover the Eurobonds issued in 2008. Unfortunately, the government did not make clear public announcements on the purposes of increasing the foreign debt of Georgia by a half billion USD. Firstly, it said that the money was needed for implementing new energy power projects, but afterwards the plans were changed, and it was said that all the money would be channeled to the Fund of Future Generations (this Fund was mainly set up for the economic rehabilitation of Abkhazia and South Ossetia after they were reintegrated in Georgia) and the Fund for Stable Development (this Fund was set up specifically for preventing crisis developments in the economy). Finally, it was said that these Funds would get only half of the money received from the Eurobondsm and a decision would be made at a later date in regards to the purpose for the other half of the amount. Thus, the government hitherto either does not know of the purpose for the increase of the country's foreign debt by a half billion USD, or it conceals its intention from the taxpayers who are to pay this debt with the relevant interest.

In April 2011, the government placed 10-year Eurobonds in the amount of $500 million with an interest rate of 7.125 percent. In parallel to placing the new bonds, Georgia bought back 83.4 percent, or $417 million worth of Eurobonds, of the 5-year $500 million Eurobonds issued in April of 2008. The fact that the Eurobonds issued were managed to be refinanced in 2008 is a positive event since it was apparent that Georgia would be unable to cover the debt and would have to refinance it. Additionally, the year of 2013 is a year for Presidential elections, whereas 2011 is a relatively quiet year in terms of politics. Moreover, 10-year Eurobonds will need to be covered in the year of 2021, which must be a politically quiet year also since the Constitutional timeframe does not require that Georgia conduct Presidential or Parliamentary elections in 2021. At the same time, the question as to on what was spent from the $500 million received from issuing Eurobonds in 2008 will remain unanswered, or why only 83.4 percent and not 100 percent of the 2008 Eurobonds was bought back by the Eurobonds issued in 2011. Unfortunately, the GoG does not make official comments on these issues.

To summarize, it can be inferred that during the Presidential and Parliamentary elections, the Government implemented several large-sized projects with doubtful economic viability (e.g., Lashkhi, Evgenidze, Narmania and Gabedava, 2008).

Chapter 5

Economic Challenges for Post-War Georgia

5.1. International Financial Support

Generally speaking, the Georgian economy stood the test of the five-day Russian-Georgian war in August 2008 (e.g., Antonenko, 2008; Cornell, 2008; Cornell and Starr, eds., 2009; Jones, 2008a; King, 2008) even though it had to deal with a number of considerable difficulties during the aftermath of the conflict (Kakulia, 2008b). First of all, the country suffered huge, direct economic damage that consisted of ruined settlements and infrastructure, combined with considerable environmental damage (e.g., Grigoriev, Kondratiev and Salikhov, 2008, pp. 92-95; Westley, 2008). Post-war Georgia faced serious difficulties and new developmental challenges (Papava, 2008f, 2009c, 2009d, 2010b).

At the conference held in Brussels under the aegis of the World Bank and the UN in October 2008, it was decided to allocate $4.55 billion in financial aid for post-war Georgia, of which $2 billion was a grant and the remainder a loan (UN, and WB, 2009). Georgia received these funds during 2008-2010, and a major part of it was spent on the liquidation of economic damage caused by the Russian military aggression towards Georgia.

A particular emphasis must be placed upon dangers created by the war in the steadiness of Georgia's banking system as well as the stability of the national currency's exchange rate. Specifically, August 11, 2008 was the most difficult day for the country's banking sector due to the anticipation associated with the further advancement of the Russian occupational forces that caused individuals and entities to start withdrawing their savings and deposits from the banks. In a few days, some $0.5 billion were withdrawn from the Georgian banking sector. In a month following the end of the war, only 30 percent of this amount was returned to the banks; the latter being a major cause of the banking crisis.

To avoid the banking crisis, the NBG, as the country's central bank, made a good decision when it renewed the opening of commercial bank refunding operations, thereby, creating a channel of relatively cheap credit resources for the country's commercial banks. At the same time, the interest rate for one-week deposit certificates was reduced from 12 percent to 10 percent (to discourage commercial banks from buying NBG securities), and the required reserves for commercial banks were reduced from 15 percent to 5 percent. By these steps, the NBG safeguarded Georgia from a major banking crisis but, at the same time, it contributed to the growth of the overall amount of money in circulation which, in turn, resulted in the growth of inflation.

Significant social problems of the IDPs from the conflict regions affected by the Russian aggression have prompted the government to assign funds for some new and additional social costs. First of all, the government is building temporary homes for people from such areas.

Another problem that had appeared in the aftermath of war was the significantly dropped inflow of foreign direct investments in Georgia. The primary reason behind the latter is that investors have been trying to make their investments in relatively safe countries under the conditions of the present global financial crisis, rather than ones like Georgia that had been seriously affected by the recent Russian aggression. The global financial crisis drove Georgians living abroad to reduce their financial aid to their relatives living in Georgia. Add to this, the country's huge foreign trade balance where imports exceed exports by four times and you will see that it came as no surprise that the stability of the lari exchange rate was shattered.

5.2. Economic Crisis and the "Paradox of War"

As recently as the spring of 2008, the potential of Georgia receiving a negative impact from the then-still-developing financial crisis in the USA (owing to the underdevelopment and relatively isolated nature of Georgia's financial market) was not as much considered inevitable as it looks now, even though the outlines of some of the present difficulties were already noticeable at that time (Akhmeteli, 2008).

After the five-day Russian-Georgian war in August 2008, and considering the global financial crisis, Georgia had come to face some new economic challenges (Corso, 2009; Giuli, 2009; Kakulia, 2008b; Narmania, 2009; Papava, 2008f, 2009c, 2009d, 2010b; Silagadze, 2010; Silagadze and Atanelashvili, 2010; Silagadze, and Gelashvili, 2009). These include, in particular, liquidating economic damage caused by the war, avoiding a crisis in the banking sector, preventing any further growth of the relatively high inflation rate and preserving the stability of the exchange rate of the national currency, the lari.

Throughout the course of 2008, all doubts regarding the negative impact of the global financial crisis upon Georgia's economy had disappeared. It must be noted that the summary economic indicators for 2008 clearly reflect the implications of both the global financial crisis and the Russian military aggression against Georgia.

To describe the present economic situation in Georgia, it is inevitable that some official statistical data must be used which, unfortunately, does not always correspond to the real facts. After the "Rose Revolution", the SDS was incorporated within the Ministry of Economic Development (an apparent indication of the existing conflict of interest), often enabling the government to manipulate statistical data for its own political benefit (Papava, 2009a, p. 11). Only in late 2009 was the SDS transformed into the National Statistics Office of Georgia. The latter had to develop into an independent institution, however, the authorities of the NBG and the Ministry of Finance and Economic Development have to be the members of its supreme body (the Board), meaning that the conflict of interests still persists (Papava, 2010d, p. 45).

According to the official statistics (see Appendix), the economic growth rate in Georgia amounted to as little as 2.3 percent in 2008, (it was 9.6 percent in 2005, 9.4 percent in 2006 and 12.3 percent in 2007), and the real GDP in 2009 was only 96.2 percent of 2008 (NSOG, 2011c). The annual inflation rate in 2008 amounted to 5.5 percent and in 2009 to 3.0 percent (NSOG, 2011a). It must be noted that, in this context, the apparent deficiency of Georgia's GDP resides in the fact that the public administration represents the biggest segment of economy, having a share in the GDP that accounted for 17 percent (Khaduri, 2009, pp. 151-152).

As far as Georgia's economic crisis is concerned, it must be noted that the crisis also has its own domestic roots, apparent in the economic policy mistakes that the post-revolutionary government has made in the aftermath of the "Rose Revolution" (Papava, 2009a; Rukhadze and Hauf, 2009). Other factors which have contributed directly to the rise of the economic crisis in Georgia should also be mentioned:

1. Huge amounts of foreign direct investments (FDIs) streamed into privatizations and acquisitions of real estate which led to an obvious misbalance in which the inflow of financial resources into the country substantially exceeded the real sector's growth rates.
2. With the government's lesser control of the developments in the construction sector, the industry became dominated by Ponzi schemes ("financial pyramids").
3. Banks incremented their lending resources by basically accumulating cheap resources from European financial markets with the majority of such resources having been loaned for construction and acquisition of consumer goods, of which 100 percent were imported into Georgia. Almost all of the imported lending resources, therefore, were used to finance the construction businesses infected by Ponzi schemes and the import of consumer goods. Obviously, such developments could not positively influence the country's economy.

In reply to the Russian aggression, the international community extended significant financial assistance to Georgia as a victim of the aggression. As it was mentioned above, at the conference held in Brussels under the aegis of the World Bank in October 2008, it was decided to allocate $4.55 billion. Georgia started the receiving these funds from the fall of 2008.

The crisis has also badly affected the national budget. In June 2009, the Parliament of Georgia approved a $300 million tax revenue cut from the national budget, accounting for 10.5 percent of all tax revenues previously planned for the fiscal year of 2009. At the same time, the national budget grew with the lion's share belonging to the abovementioned international donor assistance (CG, 2009a).

The negative effects of the Georgian economic crisis might have been far more distressing had the international community not extended a helping hand in response to the Russian military aggression. In other words, although war, by essence, is a negative phenomenon, it had a positive implication for Georgia, to a certain degree, to the extent that the country received an enormous amount of international financial assistance. This creates, therefore, a so-called "*Paradox of War*", or a situation wherein aggression creates not only negative consequences, but some positive ones as well (Papava, 2010d, p. 43, 2010e, p. 47).

Under such circumstances, the ten largest companies of Georgia had significantly reduced their production capacities, and some stopped operating entirely (Aris, 2009) thereby creating favorable conditions for the succession of a necroeconomy. Although the government periodically buys large amounts of fertilizers from Georgia's largest chemical factory, Azot, this enterprise has had to stop its production (Aris, 2009). Most surprisingly, however, these enterprises continued producing their products for the first months of 2009, in the "best" tradition of a necroeconomy and despite the obvious crisis in the Georgian economy, even though there was no demand for their output. They simply stopped their activities in April and May when the warehouses were completely filled with unwanted products (Aris, 2009).

5.3. Anti-Crisis Measures

Under a global financial crisis, the governments of different countries are normally trying to elaborate an anti-crisis program. Taking into account the fact that after the "Rose Revolution" the government was not able to come up with any serious program on economic development, it should not be surprising that there was any program in the country under the recession, which is unfortunate. Only in the beginning of 2011 did the Georgian experts prepare a program for its social and economic development (Tvalchrelidze, Silagadze, Keshelashvili and Gegia, 2011); unfortunately, there was not any response from the GoG.

What the government managed to come up with, though, is the so called "New Financial Package", mainly concerning the banking and construction sectors (CG, 2009b).

The steps made with regard to the banking sector were mutually exclusive. Namely, on the one hand, by alleviating the regulatory normatives of commercial banks, the NBG favored the emergence of additional credit resources in the country; and on the other hand, because banks have difficulties in placing their credit resources during the ongoing recession, the government made the decision on the emission of $155 million of treasury bills. In other words, the government would reduce its credit resources by $155 million that could have been used for crediting the real sector of its economy. The government spent financial resources obtained in the above manner on infrastructural projects.

The emission of treasury bonds would not serve as anti-crisis measure. Just the opposite, by reducing credit resources, it restrained the possibility of developing the real sector of Georgia's economy.

It is worth pointing out that three weeks before declaring the decision on the emission of treasury bills, the Ministry of Finance stated that they had nearly $30 million of free funds on their treasury account, and a tender was announced between banks in order to make better use of it. Consequently, they loaned the sum to the winning bank.

It is interesting that the winner was one of the most problematic banks which later bought treasury bills with the money, meaning that the government had to pay the bank the difference in interest rates for its own money. This operation seems obviously doubtful, but there was no adequate response from law-enforcement bodies.

As for the support from the construction sector, construction companies that were provided bank loans under the Tbilisi Municipality were guaranteed for the residential fund's renewal of the old Tbilisi.

Taking into account that many construction companies function on a "financial pyramid" (Ponzi scheme) principle, the aforementioned government measures preceded the initiation of bankruptcy procedures against these types of companies. Otherwise, the above support of the construction sector meant supporting "financial pyramids" in reality as well, which, in the long run, would adversely affect not only construction, but the banking sector as well, to say nothing of the inappropriate use of the corresponding funds from the city budget.

Unfortunately, the abovementioned "New Financial Package" did not envisage any measures for the improvement of the population's social conditions at all, which, as a rule, is a recommended action in a recession period in order to stimulate the demand.

As one can see, although the problem of necroeconomy in times of an economic crisis is still a very timely one, fortunately, the government's anti-crisis plans have hitherto not given any indication that the government is going to finance necroeconomic facilities.

On the other hand, it must be remembered that no official bankruptcy proceedings have been initiated to this point with respect to any of the necroeconomic enterprises of Georgia (Koberidze, 2009). Furthermore, as was noted above, the GoG provided financial assistance to the construction companies, many of which represented a Ponzi scheme.

This was nothing else but a step towards the zombie-ing of those construction companies and also of those banks that would have been extending loans to such construction companies (Papava, 2010a, 2010g).

5.4. Economic Liberty Act

In the second half of 2009, the president of Georgia offered the country the so called "Economic Liberty Act" (CG, 2009d, Papava, 2010d, pp. 44-45).

Some proposals reflected in the first draft of the Economic Liberty Act were virtually like "crushing into the open door" since similar problems in Georgia have been long resolved, and today they are not urgent at all.

According the first draft of the Economic Liberty Act, initiated by President Saakashvili, the government had to undertake guarantees not to restrict national currency convertibility, not to start pricing regulations, not to establish limitations to the foreign investors on the repatriation of the profits, not to have state owned shares in commercial banks, and not to introduce new regulatory institutions.

In the first place, this concerns the convertibility of Georgian currency, the lari. From the very first day (i.e. more than 15 years ago, in 1995) of its introduction to the country, it has been a convertible currency. Moreover, in 1997 Georgia joined article 8 of the agreement of the IMF, according to which the country undertook the obligation that lari convertibility would not be restrained, and having become the member of the World Trade Organization (WTO) in 1999 likewise obliges Georgia not to restrain lari convertibility. It has to be underlined, that international agreements stand higher than the country's legislation.

A situation was similar regarding the state regulation of prices. For more than 15 years now, the prices have been liberalized: prices on bread were last liberalized in 1996. Since then, Georgia, being a member of the WTO, has undertaken a commitment which does not allow any regulations of prices.

Georgia has had the law on investments for more than 13 years, under which an investor has unrestricted rights on the repatriation of the profits. Being a member of the WTO also makes Georgia liable for the above.

The requirement that the state must not have its share in commercial banks is hard to understand. In particular, it is not understandable as to the share of which state should not be in banks: of any state or only of the Georgian one. Today, the Georgian state does not have any share in commercial banks anyway, but there are two commercial banks that are state banks as well in the

Georgian banking reality. For instance, "VTB" is a Russian state bank, and the "International Bank of Azerbaijan" is an Azerbaijanian bank.

Saying, "No" to the introduction of new regulatory institutions (one of the requirements of the draft law) signals the fact that Georgia says, "No" to European integration, as the European market is a regulated one.

By the first draft of the Economic Liberty Act, it was also proposed to set budget parameters in advance by a non-budget legislation.

According to amendments which were proposed to be made to the Constitution of Georgia, it turns out that issues such as introducing new taxes or increasing the current tax rates must be resolved by means of the Referendum (CG, 2009c). Taking into account that nobody would agree to increase the taxes, holding the Referendum does not make any sense since the result is pretty predictable.

Tax policy, being a part of economic policy, should normally vary according to the situation. By making the abovementioned amendments to the Constitution, the Georgian state would be deprived of one of the efficient instruments of economic policy.

In the summer of 2011, the Parliament adopted the Organic Law on Economic Liberty Act, based on the constitutional amendments approved in December, related to tax increases through the referendum. According to the law, increasing the upper limit of taxes, excluding excise, or setting new taxes would only be possible through the referendum. Nonetheless, it is stated in the law that the government will have the right to request a "temporary" increase of taxes or setting new taxes only for a maximum of three years. It is nonsense as it is unbelievable for the people to vote for increasing the amount of money to be paid out of their pockets.

Besides, the law sets the following maximum limits for macroeconomic parameters: state loans as a share of GDP shall not exceed 60 percent; the share of the consolidated budget in the GDP shall not exceed 30 percent; and the share of the national budget deficit in the GDP shall not exceed 3 percent. Setting these parameters, by law, is also not justified because the parameters must be defined by economic policy. It should be noted that the current state budget does not meet the last two parameters. It is stated in the law that, in this case, the government should submit such a national budget for approval to the Parliament, containing a plan for meeting the limits. The Law on Economic Liberty Act, as well as constitutional amendments, will be in force at the end of 2013 (CG, 2011c).

Some of the above mentioned initiatives that President Saakashvili stated in 2009 are not reflected in the law. The law neither envisages any more limitations on issuing permits and licenses nor places a limit on increases associated with the number of regulating agencies. This is acceptable as there would not be a barrier for reaching an agreement of a free trade regime with EU.

Chapter 6

MISTAKES MADE BY THE IMF AND WORLD BANK IN POST-REVOLUTIONARY GEORGIA

6.1. POST-REVOLUTIONARY RENOVATIONS OF THE RELATIONS WITH THE BRETTON WOODS INSTITUTES

There is a constant discussion in academic literature as to the role and significance of the institutions of the Bretton Woods system, especially related to the IMF in the world economy and in individual countries. The question of reforming the IMF becomes especially topical after the start of each, more or less, large-scale financial crisis. This was also the case after the crisis at the end of the 1990s (e.g., Camdessus, 1999; De Gregorio, Eichengreen, Ito and Wyplosz, 1999; Eichengreen, 2000; Truman, 2006; Truman, ed., 2006; Vreeland, 2003), and this problem still continues to be discussed today (e.g., Eichengreen, 2011; Krugman, 2008, pp. 115-118; Stiglitz, 2010, pp. 210-237; Subacchi and Monsarrat, 2009, pp. 29-49; WB, 2011, pp. 76-82). The need to reform international financial institutions and the IMF, in particular, is not only acknowledged by the latter, but it has become one of the priorities in the work of the IMF under conditions of the financial crisis.

In order to work out a strategy for transforming these institutions, it is necessary to know about the mistakes that they have made in various countries of the world. In the context of a post-Communist transformation, an analysis of their activity in the countries of the FSU is of special interest (e.g., Gomulka, 1995; Zevin, 2001). Unfortunately, emphasis is usually placed on the activity of the IMF and not on that of the World Bank.

The IMF programs occupy a special place in the reform of the Georgian economy. Despite numerous miscalculations, important economic successes have been achieved in nineties of the 20th Century on the basis of these programs (see, Chapter 2).

The functions of the Bretton Woods institutions are strictly divided. The main focus of the IMF's activity is macroeconomic stability, whereas the programs of the World Bank are aimed at general economic reforms, institutional transformations, and developing infrastructure and other sectors of the economy. Despite this division into spheres of activity, certain issues simultaneously belong to the fields of macroeconomic policy and institutional transformation; these, naturally, require joint consideration.

While before the "Rose Revolution" members of the IMF mission simply offered the GoG erroneous recommendations, both the IMF and the World Bank have looked at the transformations carried out by the Georgian government (including its mistakes) since 2004 through only "rose-colored spectacles" and have seen them in a rosy light. On this basis, the mistakes of the IMF and World Bank can be called "rosy" (Papava, 2009g). It is only fair to note that such mistakes have been made not only by the Bretton Woods institutions, but by many other partners and allies of Georgia (Papava, 2008c).

After 1999, due to the inert character of the Georgian government, the international financial institutions (and they are not alone) lost hope in the ability of Georgia to return to the path of economic reform. The efforts of the Georgian government in the area of planning and implementing the national budget looked quite hopeless. Endless sequestrations made it completely obvious that the government lacked sufficient political will to fight corruption and that it was, therefore, unable to qualitatively change the situation with regard to tax collection. As a result, the IMF halted cooperation with Georgia in the summer of 2003; this also automatically led to curtailing the World Bank's problem (Khaduri, 2005b; Papava, 2005a).

It must be regarded as a special achievement of the post-revolutionary government that it acquired the necessary political potential and imposed financial order. Even in 2004, tax revenues doubled, and the growth promised to be stable. This success, accompanied by declarations of adhesion to democratic values, made a very strong impression on countries and international organizations that were friendly with Georgia. Consequently, the IMF renewed its program in Georgia, followed by an analogous decision of the World Bank.

The success in fiscal policy (before the revolution it had been the government's "Achilles' heel")—the upward leap in budgetary revenues—weakened the influence of the international financial institutions over the Georgian government. The staff of the IMF mission considered that the government was successfully coping with the mobilization of budgetary revenues and that recommendations on this matter from the IMF might even be superfluous. Furthermore, whereas before 2004 the IMF had literally prevented the Georgian government from changing the tax code, in 2004 it no longer blocked a reduction in the tax burden, which came into effect in 2005 (Khaduri, 2006).

Of special significance in this context was a conflict between the Georgian government and the heads of the IMF mission that became extremely acute in spring 2005, connected mainly with the existence of extra-budgetary accounts. This conflict culminated in the complete victory of Georgia's Prime Minister who, in May 2005, visited Washington and demanded that the IMF leadership replace the acting head of the mission. The professionalism of the mission's head could hardly be doubted: his demands had been justified. Nevertheless, he was recalled. This was a serious warning to all members of the mission and to its new head: any conflict with the Georgian government might put a sorry end to the career of any one of them. The permanent representative of the IMF in Tbilisi eventually managed to establish cooperation with the Georgian government in a form acceptable to both sides, and his stay in Georgia was extended twice (something that happens extremely rarely in IMF practice). Naturally, after this episode, members of the IMF staff did not find it in their interest to enter into serious conflict with the Georgian Government.

At the beginning of autumn 2007 the IMF program came to an end, and the government had no plans to start a new program. Only after the Russian–Georgian conflict in August 2008 did the IMF renew cooperation with the Georgian government.

6.2. "Rosy" Mistakes

6.2.1. Extra-budgetary Accounts

Almost immediately after the "Rose Revolution", extra-budgetary accounts were created in the name of the force structures; former state officials who were accused of corruption paid so-called freedom charges into these accounts after their arrest. In this way it was considered that people exposed as corrupt would return stolen money and property to the state, while the state gained an additional source of revenue. To be fair, it should be noted that only part of the "freedom charges" ended up in these accounts; the rest accumulated on the revenue side of the national budget.

It is of special importance that the spending of extra-budgetary funds was a prerogative of the government and was not subject to public oversight: information about extra-budgetary accounts was not available to Parliament, to the Chamber of Control of Georgia, or to the mass media. Only the magnitude of corresponding accruals to the national budget was known, while the volume of funds in extra-budgetary accounts was not even susceptible to expert assessment.

It is clear that such a practice cannot ensure a stable source of revenue. Initially, collections were more or less successful, but then the amounts collected from officials had declined significantly. Consequently, the government switched its attention to business, compelling businessmen to pay so-called voluntary contributions into the extra-budgetary accounts (Anjaparidze, 2006b).

It is necessary to acknowledge that the system of extra-budgetary accounts was first used in Georgia as early as 1992. One of the chief measures initiated by the IMF in the second half of 1994 was to ensure that all such accounts should either be made part of the national budget or be eliminated by 1995. Against this background, it was unexpected that the IMF should close its eyes to the reopening of such accounts after the "Rose Revolution". Unofficially, the situation was explained in the IMF as follows: "If extra-budgetary accounts will help to reduce the level of corruption in the country, then so be it!" They seemed a lesser evil by comparison with bribery. However, the IMF was mistaken in supporting the existence of a potentially corrupt and opaque institution.

Only after businessmen began to be pressed for "voluntary contributions" did the IMF demand that the Georgian government abolish extra-budgetary accounts. The greatest and most prolonged resistance to this came from the Ministry of Defense, whose extra-budgetary account was closed last in the spring of 2006. As for the World Bank, despite its work against corruption, it did not react in any way to the existence of extra-budgetary accounts.

6.2.2. Systematic Violation of Property Rights

The greatest mistake made by the post-revolutionary government has been its encroachment on the right to private property (HRIDC, 2008b). People have been compelled by pressure from the force structures to "voluntarily" cede their property to the state. This process has been carried out under the cover of so-called de-privatization, allegedly designed to correct the mistakes made in the course of privatization up to 2004 (under the Shevardnadze administration). In fact, there has been a redistribution of property in favor of businessmen who have close connections with the authorities. In this case too, however, the World Bank has not reacted in any way.

True, the permanent representative of the IMF in Tbilisi has pointed out the impermissibility of violations of property rights (Christiansen, 2006). He did so, however, in an extraordinarily mild form and his statement had no consequences of any kind.

6.2.3. The Selling of State Property

The large-scale privatization that was begun in 2004 involved the legislation violations (Gujaraidze, Barbakadze, Gujaraidze, Mchedlishvili and Kakhaberi, 2007). It is precisely by such means that Russian, Kazakh, and Arab capital has entered Georgia. Often, a contract concluded between the state and a new private owner has indicated a sum that is only a small fraction of that originally announced. In the privatization of power engineering plants, for example, the Czech company, Energo-pro, declared that it would pay $312 million for ownership rights, but later the sum indicated in the contract was just $123 million (CG, 2007c). Not infrequently, firms with dubious founders and dubious capital were created for the purpose of privatizing certain objects, and it was precisely these firms that won the corresponding tenders (Gujaraidze, 2010).

In some cases, another state became the owner of Georgian state property (for instance, after the sale of Tbilisi Gas [Tbilgaz], its owner became a state company of Kazakhstan); this cannot be considered privatization. Unfortunately, however, no one has heard the World Bank's opinion on this matter, although privatization is one of the most important issues for it.

6.2.4. Restriction of Competition

After the "Rose Revolution", state institutions started to be dismantled, thereby weakening the Georgian state. In particular, at the end of 2004, in the framework of the reforms being conducted, the state anti-monopoly service was abolished, contributing to the growing monopolization of the market.

In October 2007 at a session of the government, the president of Georgia entrusted the function of anti-monopoly regulation for the markets in salt, sugar, and other commodities to the Ministry of Internal Affairs (CG, 2007a). This is complete nonsense because this function has no connection with the work of the police or of the state security service. (Another curious incident of this sort occurred in spring 2006 when the president instructed the minister of defense to look for markets for the sale of Georgian wine.) This too, unfortunately, failed to attract the attention of the World Bank.

6.2.5. Manipulation of Statistical Data

Up until 2004, the SDS was directly subordinated to the country's president. In 2004 the department was incorporated into the Ministry of Economic Development; this is absurd because it means that the government not only works out and implements one or another economic policy but also publishes statistical information about the degree of success of this policy. As a result, the statistical service performed the same political function in post-revolutionary Georgia as it did in the Soviet Union.

In August 2006, the SDS reported that the annual inflation rate, as of July, was 14.5 percent. The NBG and the government were rightly criticized by the permanent representative of the IMF in Tbilisi. As a result, however, the government dismissed the chairman of the SDS, and the official who succeeded him was instructed by the Prime Minister to gradually "lower" the inflation indicators. The government declared that, as of December 2006, the inflation rate in Georgia had fallen to 8.8 percent; formally this satisfied the IMF requirement that the rate should not reach double figures. Apart from the government, no one in Georgia believed the official inflation estimate. The IMF not only made no protest at this "solution" to the inflation problem, but even gave a positive appraisal for the work of the NBG and of the Georgian government as a whole.

6.2.6. Populism of the Government

Unfortunately, after the revolution, the Georgian government started to carry out populist economic programs, leading in practice to rising inflation. A special place among these programs is occupied by measures that have the noble aim of increasing employment: employers are required to place unemployed people in their firms for a period of three months with the state paying their wages (see 4.3 from the Chapter 4). As a result, tens of millions have been spent from the national budget, but only a few individuals have obtained long-term employment. In the majority of cases, the employer and the unemployed person reach an understanding: the former is willing to sign any document stating that a specific person really is going to work and doing something in his firm, while the unemployed person is glad to receive $85 over three months for doing nothing. Over the winter of 2007-2008, the population was given vouchers, paid for from the national budget, for the purchase of various commodities, and the level of inflation rose even higher. Although controlling inflation is one of the most important functions of the IMF, it has not responded with any warnings to the government.

6.2.7. A Taxation Oddity

In 2006, on the initiative of the president, the 20 percent social tax and the 12 percent income tax became a single income tax set at 25 percent (CG, 2008e). The corresponding change in the taxation code entered into force in 2007. As the income tax and the social tax are calculated on different bases (the income tax is deducted from wages, whereas the social tax is based on the wage fund), it is impossible, in principle, to combine them, and it is hard to imagine the specialists at the IMF not knowing about this. In essence, the social tax on employers was abolished while the income tax on employees was increased from 12 percent to 25 percent.

6.2.8. Program to Overcome Poverty

As early as 2003, a program of economic development and poverty reduction was prepared and affirmed by the president. At that time, it had strong approval from the IMF, World Bank, and other international institutions that had actively participated in its preparation (IMF, 2003). However, the government at that time was quite incapable of functioning and did not even begin to implement this program. The new authorities, rejecting everything done before them, assigned it to oblivion for four years (Papava, 2009e). Nevertheless, both the IMF and the World Bank publicly declared that they were assisting in the implementation of a poverty reduction program in Georgia. Moreover, in September 2007, the IMF even announced that the program had been successfully completed. This was probably far from being the case, considering that, in 2008, the authorities declared a new start against the fight of poverty (Meskhia, 2008). However, it is a mere formality to call the pre-electoral program under the slogan, "A United Georgia Without Poverty!" a "program" at all, inasmuch as the document contained only adjurations, spread over several pages (CG, 2008d). Unfortunately, the poverty issue was only used by the post-revolutionary government for election purposes (Basilia, 2008).

6.2.9. A Free Economic Zone - An Economic Trap

The idea of a free economic zone (or an economic space in which privileges of various sorts are granted that do not apply in the rest of the country) is associated with the name of Aslan Abashidze, the former leader of Ajaria. Under the conditions of economic liberalization, the creation of a free economic zone is superfluous, but neither Abashidze nor the post-revolutionary government took this into account (Papava, 2007c).

The situation is complicated by the fact that the Georgian economy is currently suffering from an investment "famine". Creating a free economic zone under these conditions (the authorities have decided to first put this idea into effect in the port city of Poti) will exacerbate the shortage of investments, thereby impeding economic development as a whole. Both foreign and domestic investors will put money only into the free economic zone, meaning that the economic development of this region and the adjacent areas will take place at the rest of Georgia's expense (Patsuria, 2008).

The IMF specialists held a seminar, devoted to the negative consequences associated with creating free economic zones in countries suffering from an investment "famine", for those government ministers and members of parliament who were responsible for making economic policy. In a mild manner, they recommended that the Georgian government should not create a free economic zone, but no heed was taken of them.

Why has the IMF, in dealing with this problem, acted behind the scenes rather than publicly? After all, it had a joint program with the Georgian government that allowed it to convey its demands more firmly. As later became clear, one of the experts of the World Bank, even before the seminar was held, had given the authorities a positive recommendation in the name of the Bank: the IMF wished to avoid an institutional confrontation with the World Bank. In this way, the economic interests of Georgia received a short shrift.

In fact, the free economic zones in Georgia are not developing because of the problems related with Russian-Georgian war in August 2008, macroeconomic instability, etc. (Sakevarishvili, 2010).

6.2.10. Rejection of an Independent Central Bank

As early as spring 2006, the Georgian government intended to curtail the powers of the NBG and, to this end, prepared draft amendments to the law on the NBG, designed to transfer the function of banking oversight to an agency especially created for this purpose. These plans could not be carried out due to resistance from the officials of the NBG and from the parliamentary Committee for Finance and Budget. In spring 2008, when the president of the NBG had retired and his duties were being performed by the vice president, the government seized the moment and (despite the opposition of the parliamentary committee) deprived the NBG of the power to exercise banking oversight, leaving it as the sole function of regulating inflation. The IMF, in a memorandum, voiced the modest request not to violate the independence of the NBG. Nonetheless, no one was obliged to take any notice because, by spring 2008, the IMF no longer had a program in Georgia.

6.2.11. Emission of Eurobonds and an Increase in the Country's Foreign Debt

After the "Rose Revolution" there was stable growth in revenues to the national budget. Nevertheless, in spring 2008, the government made an emission of Eurobonds, thereby increasing the country's foreign debt by $500 million (CG, 2008b). The Georgian government has never stated the purpose of this borrowing. Thus, the taxpayers, who will have to repay 7.5 percent of the total credit each year up to 2013, remain ignorant of the plans for spending the borrowed money. Alas, neither the Georgian government nor the IMF has given any sort of explanation for this senseless emission.

6.2.12. "Green Friday"

After the "Rose Revolution", the Georgian economy began to fall sick with one of the varieties of "Dutch disease" (Nafziger, 1997, p. 335). A substantial inflow of foreign currency resulted, above all, from the growth of FDIs and from remittances (Aslamazishvili, 2006; Papava, 2005c, 2007a). In autumn 2008, with the start of the global financial crisis, these sources dried up. The Georgian–Russian military conflict in August 2008 also had a negative effect on FDIs (Kakulia, 2008b; Papava, 2008f). It became obvious that objective conditions necessitated the devaluation of the national currency. Instead of carrying out a gradual devaluation of the lari, however, the NBG held the exchange rate practically unchanged for forty days, expending a fifth of its foreign currency reserves in the process.

On Friday, November 7, 2008, the exchange rate of the dollar flew up: in the morning a dollar cost 1.44 lari; by the evening the cash machines were empty and the exchange rate at the currency exchange points stood at 1.65 although no one was selling dollars. After completion of the first deal, trading at the Interbank Currency Exchange (ICE) was halted, supposedly for technical reasons; this caused a panic (Papava, 2008b).

With four times as many imported as domestically produced goods in Georgia's consumer market, "Green Friday" brought about a rise in prices because importers did not understand what further steps the NBG would take.

In October 2008, a conference took place in Brussels under the aegis of the World Bank at which it was decided to allocate $4.55 billion in financial aid to Georgia ($2 billion as grants, the rest as loans). This money was intended to cover the economic and social losses born by Georgia as a result of the August war (CG, 2008l). For its part, the IMF also allocated $750 million for the purpose of macroeconomic stabilization (CG, 2008h). Such a substantial inflow of foreign currency, in principle, excluded the possibility of a currency crisis in Georgia, but, unfortunately, the country was not insured against a repetition of "Green Friday" (Papava, 2008a).

For Georgia, as for any other country, it is important that the international financial institutions should not only patch up holes in the national budget, but also provide competent advice. Moreover, obviously, harm is done to a country when they acquiesce in mistakes made by its government. Although I do not doubt for a second that there are qualified specialists at the IMF and World Bank, the experience of post-revolutionary Georgia bears witness to the need to reform these institutions: their work should be guided primarily by professional values and not by considerations of any other kind.

Chapter 7

EUROPEAN CHALLENGE FOR THE GEORGIAN ECONOMY

7.1. THE EU'S ECONOMIC MODEL AND GEORGIA'S PATH TO IT

It is not easy to describe the EU's economic model, which is still in formation (Fioretos, 2003). According to Albert (1991), the EU has been a battlefield for the two key models of capitalism, i.e., the Anglo-American and the "Rhenish" (German-Japanese) ones.

In the Anglo-American model, the transfer of shareholding takes place quickly and without any obstacles, stock exchanges play a key role in companies' funding, and some 40-60 percent of company shares are owned by institutional investors (such as insurance and pension providers). At the same time, the public sector is relatively small and social policy with respect to poverty and inequality is somewhat liberal; namely, inequality is understood as one of the incentives of competition, and the fight against poverty is believed not only to be the government's function, but also within the sphere of private charities as a part of moral practice and philanthropy.

In the Rhenish model, shareholding is somewhat stable and the banking sector plays a key role in funding shareholder companies. Stock markets are relatively constrained and, therefore, less active. The spheres of regulation are somewhat broad and the government's role in the distribution of the GDP, ensuring equal competition and addressing social needs, is substantial.

Remarkably, the two models have merged in a number of EU member states, under the pressure of the Anglo-American model over the Rhenish.

The EU countries do not share a *unified* economic model. Instead, there is a *common* economic model that is not yet strong enough to ensure full unification. At the same time, the integration underway in the EU is dominated by the transition from the common market to the unified market which, in turn, has paved the way for economic and currency unions.

One of the most fundamental principles of the EU is the "preservation of what has been accomplished," which is important for any membership candidate to bear in mind. Whatever has been unified and achieved on the way to the integrated model must be unconditionally copied by all candidates.

In view of continual official statements regarding Georgia's striving toward Euro-Atlantic organizations (e.g., Papava and Tokmazishvili, 2006), Georgia, at the same time, understands the tension between these two models. In particular, the Rhenish model prevails in shareholding and company funding which has yielded small and passive financial markets. This is a direct consequence of official policy. On the other hand, the spheres of regulation are quite limited, misleadingly suggesting that Georgia fits the Anglo-American model. This is most evident in the government's policy on poverty and inequality, which could be described as indifference (although sometimes inaccurately called "liberalism"). In Georgia, inequality is not the government's concern at all, whereas the alleviation of poverty has forcibly (under the government's pressure) become the headache of private charities and entrepreneurs (Papava, 2009e).

Under such circumstances, it is natural to ask: Is Georgia really headed to the EU?

Deregulation, such as reducing the number of licenses and permits, has limited the legal grounds for the government's interference with businesses. Cutting tax rates significantly eased the tax burden for businesses (Khaduri, 2006). Reducing the import tax base for agricultural produce and construction materials, as well as the reduction of the import tax rate, have made Georgia much more competitive.

The new Labor Code is revolutionary. By limiting the rights of employees, it has substantially broadened those of employers. Although this may encourage businesses to develop, it also leaves employees unprotected (Tokmazishvili and Archvadze, 2007).

These sorts of reforms resemble the Southeast Asian (Hong Kong, Singapore) and Anglo-Pacific (Australian, New Zealand, US and Canada) economic models. It should come as no surprise, therefore, if Georgian reforms track the way to the East and, in fact, they are moving toward the

American-Canadian model along the path through Southeast Asia and Australia-New Zealand.

As the Earth is round, one may eventually arrive in Europe by travelling eastward from Georgia, but one would approach Europe from a different direction! It is worth noting that following the five top nations in "Doing Business" (the Georgian government's favorite rankings list), the next five include Great Britain, Denmark, Australia, Norway and Ireland, supporting the idea that Georgia may reach the European Union from the West rather than from the East, the obviously shorter path (Papava, 2009f).

Columbus also counted on the fact that the Earth is round. To reach India, he took the opposite path and travelled west. If he had not mistaken America for India, he would have continued travelling and, most probably, would have reached the Indian shore. Like Columbus, the Georgian government has not fully realized that it is heading toward its goal in the opposite direction (Papava, 2008g).

Georgia is not the first state to make its way to the EU via this strange route. The Baltic states, especially Lithuania and Estonia, reached their goals in the same way, long before Georgia. Another indication that this path can be effective is the recently-adopted European Neighborhood Action Plan.

7.2. Transition to the Free Trade Regime with the EU

The key challenge for Georgia is to achieve some general European economic standards, as well as European standards of democratization and protection of human rights (e.g., Khidasheli, 2011a, 2011b).

For Georgia, transition from a simple or extended free trade regime (Vincentz, 2008) to a free trade regime, under the Deep and Comprehensive Free Trade Agreement (DCFTA), with the EU may become both a strong incentive and an effective mechanism to address their major challenge which consists in achieving general European economic standards (Gogolashvili, 2007; Kakulia, 2011). It will force Georgia to carry out rather effective measures to implement consistent economic reforms.

Since 2004, Georgia has cooperated closely with the EU within the framework of the European Neighborhood Policy (ENP) (e.g., Baratashvili, Sichinava and Bulia, 2010). In 2007, Georgia joined the EU's Black Sea Synergy (BSS) initiative. In 2009, Georgia also became involved in a brand new EU initiative called the Eastern Partnership (EAP) (e.g., Mkrtchyan, Huseynov and Gogolashvili, 2009; Sekarev, 2010).

The proposed transition to the free trade regime with the EU will encourage and attract some new foreign investments which, in the long run, will result in the relative acceleration of economic growth rates (Milcher and Slay, 2005). While this issue is still in its embryonic stage as the US is concerned, the EU side sees the transition to the free trade regime, as was decided by the Extraordinary European Council which met in Brussels on September 1, 2008 (CEU, 2008), as being dependent upon Georgia's meeting those conditions which Brussels has requested to be observed within the format of the EU Neighborhood Policy. These include adopting a new Labor Code that would secure the same rights for the employees as in the EU, and enacting a European-style anti-monopoly and consumer rights protecting legislation.

According to the EU's Eastern Partnership Plan, unveiled on December 3, 2008 in Brussels (CEC, 2008), the European Commission reached out to Georgia and four other former Soviet states, proposing generous financial assistance programs and free trade deals (e.g., Jowiak, 2008; Mkrtchyan, Huseynov and Gogolashvili, 2009; Sekarev, 2010).

Although the Georgian government has generally welcomed the EU's initiative regarding the CDFTA, the EU's conditions, considered by this organization as a must in order for the free trade regime become a reality, regrettably have been disregarded by the Georgian government. Neither the Letter of Intent sent by the Georgian government to the IMF on September 9, 2008, for example, nor the Memorandum of Economic and Financial Policies for 2008-2009 make any impression that, in the observable future, the Georgian government plans to amend the Labor Code and to adopt a new European-standard, anti-monopoly and consumer rights protecting legislation (IMF, 2008). To put it in other words, the Georgian government is by no means hurrying to implement a transition to the free trade regime with the EU.

The transition to the free trade regime with the EU is of vital importance for Georgia, and the Georgian government should not associate this issue with political speculations. Up until now, the government has just made illusions that it was striving to get closer to the EU. That striving, however, has only been based upon words and not actions (Papava, 2008d, 2008g, 2009f). In fact, the government has shown no intention of meeting EU requirements.

After the war with Russia, Tbilisi also received a proposal from the US administration to begin consultations on transitioning to a Georgia-US free trade regime. Because this idea is still embryonic, it is important that the US and the EU coordinate their efforts as a means of pushing the government to take consistent steps toward its integration with the West.

Finally, of no less importance may be the EU's cooperation with the IMF and the World Bank. A greater coordination of their programs may be used as an additional instrument for exerting a positive influence on the Georgian government.

7.3. Post-War Options for the New Models of Development*

After the August-2008 war with Georgia, Russia unilaterally recognized the independence of Abkhazia and South Ossetia and embarked upon setting up its own military bases in both breakaway regions of Georgia. Consequently, a new reality emerged that put Georgia in quite a different situation. Unless the status quo from before the August-2008 war is restored, Georgia will not only lose all hopes for reinstating its territorial integrity, but also will have to face the loss of its potential towards integrating into the Euro-Atlantic institutions.

Under such circumstances, there is a need to choose, based upon international experience, such a model of development which would enable the strengthening of regional security and stability, and will also ensure protection of Georgia's national interests (Gegeshidze and Papava, 2009).

Since the early 1990s, the separatist-controlled provinces of Abkhazia and South Ossetia, with the aid of Russia's indirect military assistance, succeeded to withdraw from the area of Tbilisi's control. Simultaneously, Russia obtained the status of peacekeeper within the CIS format and deployed its peacekeeping force in both regions. In fact, Moscow used its "peacekeeping force" to maintain the security of its own puppet regimes. Although Moscow officially recognized Georgia's territorial integrity when Moscow introduced a visa regime in its relations with Georgia in 2001, it did not include Abkhazia and South Ossetia in the area of application of that regime. It was the Kremlin's first step to politically separate both breakaway regions from the rest of Georgia. Afterwards, Russia granted residents in both regions with its citizenship and distributed Russian passports.

After the five-day war between Russia and Georgia in August 2008, Moscow unilaterally recognized the national independence of Abkhazia and South Ossetia. It is noteworthy that after a number of Western nations had

* The 7.3 is written with *Archil Gegeshidze*.

recognized the independence of Kosovo, the Kremlin did not even attempt to hide its own intentions regarding Georgia's breakaway regions. Moreover, before the recognition of Kosovo by the West, Moscow had repeatedly warned the world that Kosovo would have set a precedent and would, therefore, have given a green light to the recognition of national independence of separatist provinces in the post-Soviet area.

The world's leading nations strongly criticized Moscow's aggression against Georgia and the recognition for the independence of Abkhazia and South Ossetia. Despite this, it is practically unthinkable to expect that Moscow may change its decision in the foreseeable future. On the contrary, Moscow will take steps to keep its military bases there for an indefinite time. Thus, Georgia has found itself in a situation where it is likely to have a continued territorial dispute with the occupant neighbor of a part of its own territory. Obviously, Tbilisi will never reconcile to the idea that its territorial integrity has been impaired and that two of its historic provinces have been taken away from it. The situation resembles something which Europe has experienced a number of times in its recent history.

Under the present conditions, Georgia needs to come up with a new model of development based upon international experience which will respond to the best of its national interests. From this standpoint, it seems that the cases of Finland, Serbia and Cyprus are most relevant to be considered. Undoubtedly, each of these models has certain strengths and weaknesses.

Finland's experience is unacceptable for Georgia, as a matter of principle. Under an enormous military and diplomatic pressure from the Soviet Union, Finland had to make some huge concessions in order to preserve its nominal sovereignty. Specifically, in the early 1940s, as a consequence of hostilities conducted in the context of World War Two, Finland had to yield ten percent of its territory to the Soviet Union. Despite this huge price that Finland had to pay for peace, this country managed to develop a right course of political and economic development, making it one of the successful democracies of present-day Europe. This model could figuratively be labeled as the "*stick without a carrot*". For reasons of psychological character and historical memory, it is unlikely that Georgian society will reconcile itself to the fact that Abkhazia and South Ossetia are lost for good. The country, then, can make no choice regarding its future development in exchange for the loss of its territories, especially in consideration of the fact that nearly the whole world supports its territorial integrity.

Serbia's example is somewhat different. After February 2008, when the USA and the leading European nations did not heed Belgrade's opposition and recognized the independence of Kosovo, Serbia began an accelerated process of its integration into Europe. Serbia, as one of the key countries in the Balkans, was practically assured that it would be allowed to completely integrate with the European and the Euro-Atlantic organizations if this was what it wanted. Furthermore, the EU had already signed a Stability and Association Agreement with Serbia, and talks were underway about the transition of Serbia and the Schengen zone to a visa-free regime. At the same time, all were aware that, without Serbia's recognition of Kosovo's independence, Serbia's integration with the European structures would be unthinkable. Consequently, without this, no long-term peace and security may be ensured in the Balkans. In the meantime, even the most pro-Western political groups in Serbia are not yet ready to lose their hopes for the reintegration of Kosovo. This is exactly why the West has been trying to "drag" Serbia into the *Europeanization* process. The goal is to give Serbia an appetite for the intensification of this process and, so long as it faces a dilemma, eventually making this country to give up Kosovo. Again figuratively, this case resembles a "*stick with a carrot*". Although Serbia is promised to get a lot of *carrots* for this decision, such as a rapid integration with the EU, for the reason mentioned while discussing the Finnish case, is a scenario which cannot be reproduced in Georgia.

The example of Cyprus appears to be the most relevant for post-war Georgia. More than 30 years ago the northern part of the island, with a huge military assistance from Turkey, broke away from Nicosia, followed by Ankara's recognition of Northern Cyprus's independence. No other country has upheld Turkey's decision since then. Meanwhile, some strong democratic developments and market-oriented reforms in Cyprus enabled the country to grow in its wealth, to join the EU and, thereby, to become attractive to the once separatism-oriented dwellers of Northern Cyprus. In case of an eventual reunification of the island, this case will definitely qualify as a "*carrot without a stick*".

In the 21st century, the case of Cyprus might be rather promising for Georgia. The fact is that Brussels' initiatives towards Georgia are not limited to extending some financial assistance to Tbilisi. Brussels has announced its readiness to take some visa facilitation measures within the framework of the EAP Program and make a transition to a free-trade regime with Georgia, thus making Georgia's Europeanization process increasingly filled with content.

In the aftermath of the Russian aggression against Georgia and Moscow's recognition of the independence of Abkhazia and South Ossetia, the only choice for Georgia is to ensure its democratic development and sound market reforms as prompted by the Cypriot experience. Furthermore, it is recommended that the EU, within the framework of the EAP Program, ties its political support and financial assistance to Georgia with the latter's success in democratic transformation. This strategy would ensure Georgia's rapid *rapprochement* with the EU.

The US government also has to play an important role in encouraging Georgia to get closer to the EU. To this end, Washington and Brussels must work for a greater coordination of their efforts with respect to Georgia. It is recommended that the US financial assistance to Georgia be harmonized with similar EU assistance programs.

Making Georgia more EU-oriented should also be a priority for the IMF and the World Bank. The conditionality of their programs must be in full harmony with that of Brussels in relation to Georgia.

Chapter 8

In Lieu of Conclusions: Myths about Georgia's Economy

During the post-revolutionary reformation of Georgia's economy, significant experience has been accumulated in this field, both positive and negative. Any sphere of social life that is exposed to the creation of myths and economics is no exception: there are many myths, and destroying those myths is a task for economists (e.g., Hicks, Klages and Raffa, 1971; Mishan, 1986). A plethora of myths about the post-revolutionary Georgia have also been created. There are special publications aimed to mythologize the post-revolutionary economic reforms in Georgia (e.g., Burakova, 2011; ESI, 2010; Udensiva-Brenner, 2010). As usual, they have been created by politicians and have been disseminated through the mass media. Publications that help to evade the misconceptions and stereotypes (e.g., Applebaum, 2008; De Waal, 2011; Jobelius, 2011b; Lazarus, 2010; Mitchel, 2009; MacFarlane, 2011; Roubanis, 2009), including those related to economic reforms (De Waal, 2011; Jobelius, 2011a; MacFarlane, 2011; Papava, 2009a, 2011b; Rukhadze and Hauf, 2009), are very important to better understand the essence of post-revolutionary transformations associated with Georgia's economy.

The most accepted myths of Georgia's economy need to be debunked.

8.1. Myth 1: "Georgia - A Country of Neo-Liberal Reforms"

Georgia received this status thanks to the enumerated successes in reforming its economy. The adoption of the Labor Code, which limits employees' rights and expands those of employers, should be pointed out along with downsizing government employees, reducing the tax burden and simplifying the procedures for obtaining licenses and various types of permits necessary when starting up a business. Such reforms were called *neo-liberal* reforms; it was emphasized that such reforms contributed to improve the investment attractiveness of the country (Gurgenidze, 2009; Udensiva-Brenner, 2010).

Thanks to these reforms, according to *Doing Business*, which is prepared by the International Financial Corporation (IFC) and the World Bank, Georgia moved from 112th place to 37th place in 2006; to 18th place in 2007; and to 12th place in 2010 (WB, 2010). Of course, the government of the country advertises this achievement in every way possible. The actual situation is not as cheerful as represented by the rating results.

After the "Rose Revolution" there were many cases of property rights infringements in Georgia, especially those of Georgian entrepreneurs: private owners "voluntarily" gave up the rights on their property due to pressure from law enforcement ministries, or private buildings and facilities were demolished without a court ruling (HRIDC, 2008b). In many cases (but not always), the government has been cautious with regard to foreign investors as they have capabilities to attract attention to their problems from outside Georgia's borders (e.g., CG, 2011b; Kellogg, 2011). Taking also into account the absence of a judicial power, independent from the political elite of, the gross interference of the government in private business (Rukhadze and Hauf, 2009) and the general human rights violations (HRIDC, 2004, 2007), it can be confidently confirmed that the government does not hold back from applying certain *Neo-Bolshevik* (CG, 2007b) methods to the economy.

With this "detonating mixture" of *Neo-Liberal* rhetoric and a *Neo-Bolshevik* essence of economic reforms (e.g., De Waal, 2011, p. 13), the above mentioned *Doing Business* rating strongly overestimates the Georgian reality.

In our opinion, any rating must be taken with caution as the results of the rating very much depend on the methodology based on which stakeholders are interviewed in order to obtain a qualitative assessment of an event. This can be easily proved if, for comparison, we refer to the data of the *Global Competitiveness Report 2010-2011* rating, prepared by the World Economic Forum (WEF, 2011). According to this rating, the situation in Georgia is far from perfect: in its overall rating, Georgia settles at 93rd place; by ownership rights, it ranks the 116th place; by independent judicial power, it has the 104th place; and by effectiveness of anti-monopoly policy, Georgia ranks 135th place.

Not various ratings, but the statistical information, confirming that Georgia's citizens are in quite a difficult situation, gives a more adequate view of the economic condition in the country. Even by official data, 20 percent of Georgia's population lives below the poverty level and 60 percent below the median consumption (i.e. consumption of an "average" household) level. According to experts' evaluation, 86 percent of the population experiences serious social difficulties (Giorkhelidze, 2010, p. 40).

8.2. MYTH 2: "GEORGIA - A COUNTRY FREE OF CORRUPTION"

After a widespread combat against corruption immediately after the "Rose Revolution" which lead to success in the budgetary sphere, the electricity sector and patrol police started nurturing the myth, not without the government's participation, that the country had become completely free of corruption.

It is true that widespread petty corruption has been minimized. Nonetheless, the situation with regard to the elite corruption, which transformed from simple bribing into more complex forms, is far more complicated. However strange it might seem, actively combating against corruption contributed to this. Specifically, when former high officials and their relatives suspected in corruption paid ransom for their freedom, those payments did not go solely to the national budget. Actually, extra-budgetary accounts were established at the law enforcement bodies (State Prosecutor's Office, Ministry of Internal Affairs, and Ministry of Defense) immediately after the "Rose Revolution" and a part of the payments were channeled to those accounts. As no one exercised monitoring over those accounts, it is not known how much money was accumulated and how these funds were spent.

It is obvious that such measures, as collecting ransom for freedom, have a one-time effect. In the best case, it can be used again but with lesser outcomes. Thus, businessmen were then forced to make contributions to those accounts. Only after this did the IMF request the GoG to abolish such funds. The GoG agreed to abolish such accounts but not immediately (Anjaparidze, 2006b).

The practice of "voluntary contributions" by businesses at the request of the government is a characteristic component of post-revolutionary corruption schemes (Khutsidze, 2004).

The de-privatization process, or the review of results associated with privatization and repeated privatization, started after the Revolution in Georgia. The law enforcement ministries made owners of privatized enterprises by using intimidation to "voluntarily" give up their property to the government (CG, 2007d).

De-privatization contains a threat of repetition. Those who were deprived of their property might become willing to seek revenge, and if opposing political parties come to power the country might be caught in a vicious circle of de-privatization (Papava, 2006b).

As for the privatization, this process might be characterized as non-transparent, providing fertile soil for corruption (Gujaraidze, 2010; Gujaraidze, Barbakadze, Gujaraidze, Mchedlishvili and Kakhaberi, 2007).

8.3. Myth 3: "Georgia - A Country with No Economic Relations with Russia"

The Russian-Georgian confrontation reached its climax during the Russo-Georgian war in August 2008 (e.g., Cornell and Starr, eds., 2009), after which the formal diplomatic relations between the two countries were halted. In the post-war period there was an impression that all types of economic relations between Russia and Georgia had been terminated. This, of course, was not true because Georgia continues to "export" its labor to Russia, and Russia in turn remains among the leading investors in Georgia.

Trade between Russia and Georgia had declined markedly as tensions between the two nations have risen, though by no means ended. During this period, Russia's share of Georgia's total exports dropped from 17.8 percent in 2005 (i.e., Russia imposed bans on Georgian products a year before) to 2.0 percent, and 2.2 percent in 2008 and 2010, respectively (NSOG, 2011b). The same negative trend could be observed in imports to Georgia from Russia as well, which fell from 15.4 percent in 2005 to 6.7 percent in 2008. Russia accounted for only 5.5 percent of all imports in 2010 (NSOG, 2011b). Although it is worth pointing out that according to data on trade turnover between Georgia and Russia, the latter ranks fifth among Georgia's top trade partners (after Turkey, Azerbaijan, Ukraine and Germany but, at the same time, ahead of countries like the US, Bulgaria, China and others) (NSOG, 2011b).

Remittances are an important source of transfer income. Georgians who obtained Russian citizenship and live and work in Russia send part of their earnings back to Georgia to their relatives. Introducing a visa regime with Georgia, as well as the persecution of ethnic Georgians' (including Russian citizens) living in Russia in 2006 (Papava, 2007b), facilitated a further increase in the use of banking channels. As the banking sector developed, remittance through formal channels was gradually given the preference over other informal alternatives that used to be extremely popular in the post-Soviet sphere (such as sending money back home through intermediaries returning to their homeland) (Kakulia, 2007). Even the Russian-Georgian war in August 2008 has not impacted the choice between informal and formal channels.

In particular, in 2005 (i.e., one year before the persecution of Georgians in Russia), remittances to Georgia totaled \$403 million, with over \$240 million coming from Russia (59.6 percent of the total). In 2008, the transfers increased 2.5 times, reaching \$1,008 million. Remittances from Russia grew 2.6 times and amounted to nearly \$634 million, thus making up 63.3 percent of the total (NBG, 2011). In 2009, due to the global financial crisis, money transfers to Georgia (\$842 million in total) accounted for 84 percent of the remittance amounts received in 2008. The Russian economy was hit extremely hard by the crisis, affecting the amount of remittances sent to Georgia as well. In 2009, transfers from Russia totaled \$450 million – only 71 percent of the sum remitted a year before (the share of remittances from Russia to Georgia was still over half of the entire sum at 53.5 percent) (NBG, 2011). In 2010 compared to 2009, remittances to Georgia increased up to \$940 million as a whole. \$530 million was transferred just from Russia, increasing its total share up to 56.4 percent (NBG, 2011).

The assessment of the Russian (and not only Russian) investments in the Georgian economy proves more complicated, the reason being the easily manipulated and flawed data that prevents making any definite conclusions about the real situation. Many firms engaged in direct investments are registered in an offshore zone so that it is virtually impossible to conceal the real owners of a business and to trace the cash flows. In this regard, according to the official statistics, Russia, behind the Netherlands and the United States, is ranked third in the FDI in Georgia in 2010 (CG, 2011a).

8.4. Myth 4: "Georgia - A Country of European Orientation"

Georgia was not hiding its pro-Western orientation even before the "Rose Revolution" (e.g., Rondeli, 2001), but this became more obvious in the post-revolutionary period. Aspirations to NATO were especially emphasized. Ambition to join the EU was also not hidden (Gogolashvili, 2011).

Brussels has made significant steps towards establishing and deepening cooperation with some post-Soviet countries, including Georgia (e.g., Khaduri, 2010b). Thus, Georgia has been closely cooperating with the EU under the European Neighborhood Policy since 2004, under Black Sea Synergy since 2007, and within the framework of the Eastern Partnership since 2009 (e.g., Gogolashvili, 2011; Mkrtchyan, Huseynov and Gogolashvili, 2009; Sekarev, 2010).

Officially, Georgia actively promotes its European orientation, but, when it comes to making actual steps, the decisions of the government are inadequate, to say the least.

Thus, after the Russian-Georgian armed conflict of August 2008, the Extraordinary European Council held a meeting already on September 1, 2008 in support of Georgia, and Georgia was offered the DCFTA for a free trade regime with EC, provided that Georgia met certain conditions necessary for uniting economic areas (CEU, 2008). Specifically, Brussels requested that Tbilisi adopt a European type, anti-monopoly legislation (anti-monopoly regulations were abolished after the "Rose Revolution"), a food safety legislation that was suspended after the Revolution (Kemkhadze, 2007), and an amendment to the Labor Code so that rights of employees would be protected. Though Tbilisi welcomed these suggestions from Brussels, the GOG signed a Memorandum with IMF after several days, taking responsibility not to undertake these institutional reforms in near future (IMF, 2008). The IMF mainly focuses on maintaining macroeconomic stability, and the World Bank deals with institutional reforms. Thus, we can infer that a respective clause in the Memorandum was initiated by GoG, not the IMF.

Only in 2011 did the food safety regulations became effective again, and discussions regarding the preparation of drafting an anti-monopoly law have just been started (Kutivadze, 2011; Sakevarishvili, 2011). Discussions about amendments to the Labor Code have not started yet.

The United States-Georgia Charter on Strategic Partnership was adopted in January 2009, discussing a possibility of reaching a Free Trade Agreement

(CG, 2009e). The conditions of Brussels for a free trade regime with EC are known, but Tbilisi has basically not made any efforts to at least find out what Washington's conditions are regarding the similar issue.

At the same time, the GoG has become more and more "fascinated" not by the West, but by the East. First of all, the GoG is attracted by Singapore's experience (CG, 2008e) as well as that of Dubai and Hong Kong (CG, 2010a). According to President Saakashvili, Georgia's economy must be developed by using Singapore's model (CG, 2010c). "The European track" is mentioned in statements such as, "Georgia must become Switzerland with elements of Singapore," in the best case (CG, 2010b). Furthermore, significant differences among the economic models, as well as institutional arrangements of these countries, are completely ignored (Israelian, 2011, p. 41), to say nothing about the fact that Singapore's model is unlikely to be useful for Georgia (Dumienski, 2011). Moreover, such developed countries do not match up with the European choice declared (Mitchell, 2010). The GoG further moves the country from EU and generally from the European types of economies by taking the path of "Singaporization" (Papava, 2008g, 2009f).

To stake on Singapore, a country with authoritarian regimes of governing, the Government of Georgia underlines that the neo-liberal character of its economy and the absence of such regulations which Brussels requires from Tbilisi for introducing a free trade regime (Maksoeva, 2010, p. 40). Such views regarding Singapore's economy are far from a reality as this country has fully operating food safety institutions (e.g., AFVAS, 2011) as well as anti-monopoly regulations (CCS, 2010).

It must be noted that the interest to the so-called "Singaporization" of the economy (and of the whole country), as well as the president of Georgia, is shared by the president of Belorussia (e.g. Shveits, 2011).

Some positive expectations are connected with the Joint Declaration of the Warsaw Eastern Partnership Summit (September 29-30, 2011), according to which the EU could start talks with Georgia on DCFTA by the end of 2011, "provided sufficient progress has been made in fulfilling a number of remaining key recommendations" (EPC, 2011, p. 3).

Appendix: Macroeconomic Statistical Indicators of Georgia

Economic activity	2000	2001	2002	2003	2004	2005	2006	2007	2008	2009	2010
Nominal GDP (mln. GEL)	6 043	6 674	7 456	8 564	9 824	11 621	13 790	16 994	19 075	17 986	20 791
Nominal GDP (mln.USD)	3 060	3 219	3 400	3 991	5 125	6 411	7 762	10 172	12 801	10 767	11 663
GDP per capita (GEL)	1 368	1 517	1 705	1 972	2 277	2 689	3 133	3 867	4 353	4 101	4 687
GDP per capita (USD)	693	731	778	919	1 188	1 484	1 764	2 315	2 921	2 455	2 629
GDP growth (percent)	1.8	4.8	5.5	11.1	5.9	9.6	9.4	12.3	2.3	-3.8	6.4
Inflation (percent)	4.6	3.4	5.4	7.0	7.5	6.2	8.8	11.0	5.5	3.0	11.2
External balances											
Export (mln. USD)	323	318	346	461	647	866	936	1 232	1 495	1 134	1 575
Import (mln. USD)	709	753	796	1 141	1 846	2 488	3 675	5 212	6 302	4 500	5 156
Trade balance (mln. USD)	-386	-435	-450	-680	-1 199	-1 622	-2 379	-3 980	-4 806	-3 367	-3 581
Foreign Direct Investment (mln. USD)	131	110	167	340	499	450	1 190	2 015	1 564	658	815
Foreign Direct Investment to GDP (percent)	4.3	3.4	4.9	8.5	9.7	7.0	15.3	19.8	12.2	6.1	7.0

Appendix (Continued)

Fiscal balances & State debt	2000	2001	2002	2003	2004	2005	2006	2007	2008	2009	2010
Revenues of consolidated budget (mio. GEL)	920	1 064	1 144	1 345	2 267	2 829	3 850	4 973	5 854	5 265	5 866
Expenditures (mio. GEL)	1 136	1 029	1 114	1 261	1 836	2 426	2 979	4 379	5 411	5 397	5 480
Proficit / Deficit (-)	-216	-32	-156	-75	78	162	366	53	-383	-1 174	-935
State Debt (end of period, mio. GEL)	5 163	4 450	4 843	4 608	4 307	4 076	3 855	3 920	5 154	6 225	6 979
Exchange Rate											
GEL/USD (in average)	1.98	2.07	2.19	2.15	1.92	1.81	1.78	1.67	1.49	1.67	1.78

REFERENCES

Abesadze, R., 2011. "Some Theoretical Aspects of Economic Development." *The Caucasus and Globalization*, Vol. 5, Iss. 1-2.

Abesadze, R., and V. Burduli, 2009. "Innovative Activities and their Coordination under Advancing Globalization." *The Caucasus and Globalization*, Vol. 3, Iss. 4.

Abesadze, R., and E. Kakulia, 2009. "The Problems of State Regulation of Small Business in Georgia." *Central Asia and the Caucasus and Globalization*, No. 6 (60).

Adamescu, A. A., and E. D. Silaev, eds., 1973. *The Transcaucasian Economic Region. Economic and Geographical Essay*. Moscow: Nauka Publishers. (In Russian.)

Achelashvili, M., 2011. "On the Institutional Infrastructure of Economic Growth Management in the Post-Communist Capitalist Countries." *The Caucasus and Globalization*, Vol. 5, Iss. 1-2.

Achelashvili, M., and K., Achelashvili, 2008. "Regional Economic Policy and Growth (A Case Study of Georgia)." *The Caucasus and Globalization*, Vol. 2, Iss. 2.

Adams, W., and J. W. Brock, 1993. *Adam Smith Goes to Moscow. A Dialogue on Radical Reform*. Princeton, NJ: Princeton University Press.

Adams, D. W., and D. A. Fitchett, eds., 1992. *Informal Finance in Low-Income Countries*. Boulder: Westview Press.

AFVAS (Agri-Food and Veterinary Authority of Singapore), 2011. *Always Dependable. AVA Annual Report 2009/2010*. Singapore: Agri-Food and Veterinary Authority of Singapore, online at http://www.ava.gov.sg/NR/rdonlyres/0676D1EB-C401-4038-9D8D-84A01B52DD27/18268/ava0910_corporate.pdf.

Akhmeteli, N., 2008. "Will the American Economic Crisis Hit Georgia?" *Investor.ge*, April 2, online at http://www.investor.ge/issues/2008_2/01.htm.

Albert, M., 1991. *Capitalisme contre capitalisme*. Paris: Editions du Seuil.

Anjaparidze, Z., 2006a. "Critics Press for Improved Judicial Independence in Georgia." *Eurasia Daily Monitor, The Jamestown Foundation*, Vol. 3, Issue 81, April 26, online at http://www.jamestown.org/single/?no_cache=1andtx_ttnews%5Bswords%5D=8fd5893941d69d0be3f378576261ae3eandtx_ttnews%5Bany_of_the_words%5D=Anjaparidze%2C%20Zaalandtx_ttnews%5Bpointer%5D=1andtx_ttnews%5Btt_news%5D=31620andtx_ttnews%5BbackPid%5D=7andcHash=7cb96dfc73.

Anjaparidze, Z., 2006b. "Georgian Government Questioned about Secret Funds." *Eurasia Daily Monitor, The Jamestown Foundation*, Vol. 3, Issue 71, April 12, online at http://www.jamestown.org/single/?no_cache=1andtx_ttnews%5Bswords%5D=8fd5893941d69d0be3f378576261ae3eandtx_ttnews%5Bany_of_the_words%5D=Anjaparidze%2C%20Zaalandtx_ttnews%5Bpointer%5D=1andtx_ttnews%5Btt_news%5D=31572andtx_ttnews%5BbackPid%5D=7andcHash=864959a53b.

Anjaparidze, Z., 2006c. "Russia Continues to Press Georgian Wine Industry." *Eurasia Daily Monitor, The Jamestown Foundation*, Vol. 3, Issue 77, April 20, online at http://www.jamestown.org/single/?no_cache=1andtx_ttnews%5Bswords%5D=8fd5893941d69d0be3f378576261ae3eandtx_ttnews%5Bany_of_the_words%5D=Anjaparidze%2C%20Zaalandtx_ttnews%5Bpointer%5D=1andtx_ttnews%5Btt_news%5D=31602andtx_ttnews%5BbackPid%5D=7andcHash=0fd9fc187d.

Antonenko, O., 2005. "Frozen Uncertainty: Russia and the Conflict over Abkhazia." In *Statehood and Security: Georgia after the Rose Revolution*, B. Coppieters, and R. Legvold, eds. Cambridge: The MIT Press.

Antonenko, O., 2008. "A War with No Winners." *Survival*, Vol. 50, No. 4.

Applebaum, A., 2008. "Getting Past Mythmaking in Georgia." The *Washington Post*, November 20, online at http://www.washingtonpost.com/wp-dyn/content/article/2008/11/19/AR2008111903533.html.

Areshidze, I., 2007. *Democracy and Autocracy in Eurasia: Georgia in Transition*. East Lansing: Michigan State University Press.

Aris, B, 2009. "Donor Money Keeps Georgia Afloat." *bne—businessneweurope*, July 22, online at http://www.bne.eu/story1693/Donor_money_keeps_Georgia_afloat.

Asatiani, R., 1998. "Issues of Economic Development of the Caucasus." *Caucasica. The Journal of Caucasian Studies*, Vol. 1.

Asatiani, R., 2007. "The Phenomenon of Globalization and Its Influence on National Economies (A Case Study of Georgia)." *The Caucasus and Globalization*, Vol. 1 (3).

Asatiani, R., 2009a. "Caucasus and Georgian Economy: Past, Present, Prospects." *Current Politics and Economics of the Caucasus Region*, Vol. 2, Issue 4.

Asatiani, R., 2009b. "Post-Communist Transition Period in the Georgian Economy." *The Caucasus and Globalization*, Vol. 3, Iss.2-3.

Ascherson, N., 2004. "After the Revolution." *London Review of Books,* Vol. 26, No. 5, online at http://www.lrb.co.uk/v26/n05/neal-ascherson/after-the-revolution.

Aslamazishvili, N., 2005. "Structure and Dynamics of Foreign Investments in Georgia." *Georgian Economic Trends*, No. 3, December, online at http://www.geplac.ge/files/10150_9_706303_ec_trends_dec2005_en.pdf.

Aslamazishvili, N., 2006. "'Dutch Disease' in Georgian Economy: Current Reality and Potential Threats." *Georgian Economic Trends*, October, online at http://www.geplac.ge/files/english_october_2006.pdf.

Åslund, A., 1995. *How Russia Became a Market Economy.* Washington, D.C.: The Brookings Institution.

Åslund, A., 2002. *Building Capitalism. The Transformation of the Former Soviet Bloc.* Cambridge: Cambridge University Press.

Åslund, A., 2005. *Putin's Decline and America's Response.* Carnegie Endowment for International Peace Policy Brief No. 41, August, Washington, D.C.: Carnegie Endowment for International Peace.

Åslund, A., 2007. *How Capitalism Was Built: The Transformation of Central and Eastern Europe, Russia, and Central Asia.* New York: Cambridge University Press.

Asmus, R. D., 2010. A Little War that Shook the World: Georgia, Russia, and the Future of the West. New York: Palgrave and Macmillan.

Balcerowicz, L., 1994. "Poland, 1989–92." In *Political Economy of Economic Reform*, J. Williamson, ed. Washington, D.C.: Institute for International Economics.

Balcerowicz, L., 1995. *Socialism, Capitalism, Transformation.* Budapest: CEU.

Balzer, H., 2005."The Putin Thesis and Russian Energy Policy." *Post-Soviet Affairs*, Vol. 21, No. 3.

Baran, Z., 2004. "Removing the Thorn in Georgia's Rose Revolution." *The National Interest.* 2004, 24, March, online at http://nationalinterest.org/article/removing-the-thorn-in-georgias-rose-revolution-2604.

Baratashvili, E., A. Sichinava, and L. Bulia, 2010. "Social and Economic Aspects of EU-Georgia Relations under the European Neighborhood Policy." *The Caucasus and Globalization*, Vol. 4, Iss. 3-4.

Basilia, T., 2008. "The Issues of Poverty Measurement in Georgia." *Georgian International Journal of Science and Technology*, Vol. 1, Issue 3.

Beridze, T., 2005. "Measuring Georgia's Nonobserved Economy." *Problems of Economic Transition*, Vol. 48, No. 4.

Beridze, T., 2007. "National Economic Model: An Alternative to Globalization?." *The Caucasus and Globalization*, Vol. 1 (3).

Beridze, T., 2009. "On the Logic of the Development of the August (2008) Conflict in Georgia." *The Caucasus and Globalization*, Vol. 3, Iss. 4.

Beridze, T., and V. Papava, 2003. "The Main Macroeconomic Tendencies of Georgia in 1995–2002." In *Central Asia and South Caucasus Affairs: 2003*, Rumer, and Lau S. Y., eds. Tokyo: The Sasakawa Peace Foundation.

Berulava, I., 2010. "The Competitiveness of Human Resources: Evidence from Georgia." *The Caucasus and Globalization*, Vol. 4, Iss. 1-2.

Bezemer, D., and J. Davis, 2003. *The Rural Non-farm Economy in Georgia: Overview of Findings*. Natural Resource Institute Report No. 2729, online at http://papers.ssrn.com/sol3/papers.cfm?abstract_id=695268.

Birch, J., 1996. "The Georgian/South Ossetian Territorial and Boundary Dispute." In *Transcaucasian Boundaries*, J. F. R. Wright, S. Goldenberg, and R. Schofield, eds. New York: St. Martin's Press.

Bugajski, J., 2010. *Georgian Lessons: Conflicting Russian and Western Interests in the Wider Europe*. Washington, D.C.: Center for Strategic and International Studies.

Bunce, V., 1999. "The Political Economy of Postsocialism." *Slavic Review*, Vol. 58, No. 4.

Burakova, L., 2011. *Why it happened in Georgia*. Moscow: United Press. (In Russian.)

Burduli, V., 2007. "The Role of Globalization in Reviving the Economy of Countries in Transition (A Case Study of Georgia)." *The Caucasus and Globalization*, Vol. 1 (3).

Burduli, V., 2008. "The Potential of Higher Investment Activity in Georgia." *The Caucasus and Globalization*, Vol. 2, Iss. 4.

Burduli, V., and N. Arevadze, 2010. "Regional Factors of Employment Growth and their Influence on Economic Development (Georgian Case Study)." *The Caucasus and Globalization*, Vol. 4, Iss. 1-2.

Burkadze, V., 2007. "Structural Adjustments of the Georgian Agricultural Sector." *Georgian Economic Trends*, July, online at http://www.geplac.ge/newfiles/GeorgianEconomicTrends/2007/english-july%201.pdf.

Camdessus, M., 1999. *From Crisis to a New Recovery*. Washington, D.C.: IMF.

CCS (Competition Commission of Singapore), 2010. *Regulations*. Singapore: The Competition Commission of Singapore, online at http://app.ccs.gov.sg/legislation_Regulations.aspx.

CEC (Commission of the European Communities), 2008. *Communication from the Commission to the European Parliament and the Council. Eastern Partnership, SEC(2008) 2974/3*. Brussels: Commission of the European Communities, online at http://ec.europa.eu/external_relations/eastern/docs/sec08_2974_en.pdf.

Cecire, M., 2011. "Georgia's Democratic Stagnation Threatens Its Legitimacy." *World Politics Review*, July 12, online at http://www.worldpoliticsreview.com/articles/9446/georgias-democratic-stagnation-threatens-its-legitimacy.

CEU (Council of the European Union), 2008. *Extraordinary European Council, Brussels, 1 September, 2008, 12594/08*. Presidency Conclusions. Brussels: Council of the European Union, online at http://www.consilium.europa.eu/ueDocs/cms_Data/docs/pressData/en/ec/102545.pdf.

CG (Civil Georgia), 2005. "Newspaper: Government Controls Editorial Policies of the Private TV Stations." *Civil.Ge, Daily News Online*, February 28, online at http://www.civil.ge/eng/article.php?id=9202.

CG (Civil Georgia), 2006a. "IMF Warns Georgia on Inflation." *Civil.Ge, Daily News* Online, August 19, online at http://www.civil.ge/eng/article.php?id=13350.

CG (Civil Georgia), 2006b. "Saakashvili Comments on Motives Behind Cabinet Reshuffle." *Civil.Ge, Daily News Online,* November 10, online at http://www.civil.ge/eng/article.php?id=14053.

CG (Civil Georgia), 2006c. "Saakashvili Unveils New Economic Initiatives." Civil.Ge, Daily News Online, August 5, online at http://www.civil.ge/eng/article.php?id=13256.

CG (Civil Georgia), 2007a. "Curb Monopolies to Prevent Price Hikes – Saakashvili Tells Ministers." *Civil.Ge, Daily News Online,* October 24, online at http://civil.ge/eng/article.php?id=16088.

CG (Civil Georgia), 2007b. "Opposition Concerned over 'Property Rights Abuse'." *Civil.Ge, Daily News Online,* January 29, online at http://www.civil.ge/eng/article.php?id=14526.

CG (Civil Georgia), 2007c. "Opposition Files Questions Ahead of President's Annual Address." *Civil.Ge, Daily News Online,* March 14, online at http://www.civil.ge/eng/article.php?id=14783.

CG (Civil Georgia), 2007d. "Opposition Steps Up Criticism, Amid Ombudsman's Report." *Civil.Ge, Daily News Online,* May 25, online at http://www.civil.ge/eng/article.php?id=15174.

CG (Civil Georgia), 2008a. "Controversy over Proposed Central Bank Reform." *Civil.Ge, Daily News Online*, February 8, online at http://www.civil.ge/eng/article.php?id=17063.

CG (Civil Georgia), 2008b. "Georgia Issues Debut Bonds." *Civil.Ge, Daily News Online,* April 13, online at http://www.civil.ge/eng/article.php?id=17570.

CG (Civil Georgia), 2008c. "Georgia Starts Eurobonds Road-Show." *Civil.Ge, Daily News Online,* April 2, online at http://www.civil.ge/eng/article.php?id=17503.

CG (Civil Georgia), 2008d. "Government's Five-Year Program." *Civil.Ge, Daily News Online*, January 31, online at http://www.civil.ge/eng/article.php?id=17030.

CG (Civil Georgia), 2008e. "Government Pushes Economic Package in Parliament." *Civil.Ge, Daily News Online,* January 28, online at http://www.civil.ge/eng/article.php?id=17004.

CG (Civil Georgia), 2008f. "Government Unveils 50-Day Action Plan." *Civil.Ge, Daily News Online*, February 20, online at http://www.civil.ge/eng/article.php?id=17157.

CG (Civil Georgia), 2008g. "Gulf Emirate to Develop Free Economic Zone in Poti." *Civil.Ge, Daily News Online*, April 14, online at http://www.civil.ge/eng/article.php?id=17577.

CG (Civil Georgia), 2008h. "IMF, Georgia Agree on USD 750 mln Loan." *Civil.Ge, Daily News Online,* September 3, online at http://civil.ge/eng/article.php?id=19386.

CG (Civil Georgia), 2008i. "MP Calls for U.S. Intervention to Stop Railway Privatization." *Civil.Ge, Daily News Online,* February 19, online at http://www.civil.ge/eng/article.php?id=17148.

CG (Civil Georgia), 2008j. "Public Defender Tells Saakashvili to Make Positive U-Turn." *Civil.Ge, Daily News Online*, January 14, online at http://www.civil.ge/eng/article.php?id=16894.

CG (Civil Georgia), 2008k. "Saakashvili Praises Cabinet, Reports on 50-Day Action Plan." *Civil.Ge, Daily News Online*, March 31, online at http://www.civil.ge/eng/article.php?id=17488.

CG (Civil Georgia), 2008l. "USD 4.55 bln Aid Package Priorities." *Civil.Ge, Daily News Online*, October 23, online at http://civil.ge/eng/article.php?id=19811.

CG (Civil Georgia), 2009a. "Budgetary Amendments Unveiled." *Civil.Ge, Daily News Online,* June 17, online at http://www.civil.ge/eng/article.php?id=21128andsearch=budget.

CG (Civil Georgia), 2009b. "Government Offers New Plan to Boost Economy." *Civil.Ge, Daily News Online*, June 30, online at http://www.civil.ge/eng/article.php?id=21180.

CG (Civil Georgia), 2009c. "MPs Endorse Referendum on Tax Increase with First Reading." *Civil.Ge, Daily News Online*, December 25, online at http://www.civil.ge/eng/article.php?id=21835.

CG (Civil Georgia), 2009d. "Saakashvili Lays Out 'Act on Economic Freedom'." *Civil.Ge, Daily News Online*, October 6, online at http://www.civil.ge/eng/article.php?id=21541.

CG (Civil Georgia), 2009e. "United States-Georgia Charter on Strategic Partnership." *Civil.Ge, Daily News Online*, January 9, online at http://www.civil.ge/eng/article.php?id=20249.

CG (Civil Georgia), 2010a. "Saakashvili: Georgia will be Like Dubai in 5-7 Years." *Civil.Ge, Daily News Online*, June 22, online at http://www.civil.ge/eng/article.php?id=22438.

CG (Civil Georgia), 2010b. "Saakashvili: 'Georgia Switzerland with Elements of Singapore'." *Civil.Ge, Daily News Online*, March 9, online at http://www.civil.ge/eng/article.php?id=22064.

CG (Civil Georgia), 2010c. "Saakashvili on Ruling Party's Vision." *Civil.Ge, Daily News Online*, June 15, online at http://www.civil.ge/eng/article.php?id=22422.

CG (Civil Georgia), 2011a. "2010 FDI Down 16% to USD 553 mln." *Civil.Ge, Daily News Online*, March 11, online at http://www.civil.ge/eng/article.php?id=23232.

CG (Civil Georgia), 2011b. "Israel Protests 'Maltreatment' of Two of its Citizens in Georgian Jail." *Civil.Ge, Daily News Online*, September 22, online at http://www.civil.ge/eng/article.php?id=23955.

CG (Civil Georgia), 2011c. "Revised 'Economic Liberty Act' Passed with Final Reading." *Civil.Ge, Daily News Online*, July 1, online at http://www.civil.ge/eng/article.php?id=23691.

Chappell, P., 1990. "The Assault on Fiscal Privilege: A Simpler System with Lower Tax Rates." In *P. Chappell, J. Kay, and B. Robinson. Which Road to Fiscal Neutrality?* London: IEA.

Charap, S., and C. Welt, 2011. *A More Proactive U.S. Approach to the Georgia Conflicts*. Center for American Progress, February, online at http://www.americanprogress.org/issues/2011/02/pdf/georgia-report.pdf.

Chase, H., 2002. "Future Prospects of Caucasian Energy and Transportation Corridor. The Role of Caucasian Energy Corridor in European Energy Security." *Georgian Economic Trends*, No. 3, online at http://www.geplac.ge/publicat/economic/archives/get02n3e.pdf.

Chkhartishivili D., R., Gotsiridze, and B. Kitsmarishvili, 2004. "Georgia: Conflict Regions and Economies." In *From War Economies to Peace Economies in the South Caucasus*, P. Champain, D. Klein, and N. Mirimanova, eds. London: International Alert.

Chocheli, V., 2003. "'Syndrome of Shadow Economy:' Low Tax Burden—Low Rate of Economic Growth." *Proceedings of the Georgian Academy of Sciences—Economic Series,* Vol. 11, No. 1–2. (In Georgian.)

Chocheli, V., and V. Papava, 2005. "Global Exchange Rate Instability and Its Implications for Georgia." *Problems of Economic Transition*, Vol. 48, No. 4.

Christiansen, R. E., 2006. "Property Rights, Institutions and Growth: Will Georgia Make the Transition?," Presentation Delivered at Cato Conference, *International Monetary Fund, Resident Representative Office in Georgia*, October 27, online at http://www.imf.ge/view2.php?lang=1andview=239.

Chubais, A., 2003. "Russia's Mission in the 21st Century." *Nezavisimaya gazeta*, October 1, online at http://www.ng.ru/printed/ideas/2003-10-01/1_mission.html.

Chubais, A., 2008. "Afterword to the Unified Energy Systems of Russia." *Vestnik Evropy*, Vol. XXIV. (In Russian.)

Coppieters, B., 2003. "War and Secession: A Moral Analysis of the Georgian-Abkhaz Conflict." In *Contextualizing Secession: Normative Studies in Comparative Perspective*, B. Coppieters, and R. Sakwa, eds. Oxford: Oxford University Press.

Coppieters, B., and R. Legvold, eds., 2005. *Statehood and Security: Georgia after the Rose Revolution*. Cambridge: The MIT Press.

Cordonnier, C., 2008. "Private Savings, Macroeconomic Stability and Financial Sector Development in Georgia." *Georgian Economic Trends*,

October, online at http://www.geplac.ge/newfiles/GeorgianEconomic Trends/2008/October%202008%20(eng).pdf.

Cornell, S. E., 2001. *Small Nations and Great Powers. A Study of Ethnopolitical Conflict in the Caucasus.* Surrey: Curzon Press.

Cornell, S. E., 2002. "Autonomy as a Source of Conflict: Caucasian Conflicts in Theoretical Perspective." *World Politics*, Vol. 54, No. 2.

Cornell, S. E., 2008. "War in Georgia, Jitters All Around." *Current History,* Vol. 107, Issue 711, online at http://www.silkroadstudies.org/new/docs/publications/2007/0810CH.pdf.

Cornell, S. E., and S. F. Starr, eds., 2009. *The Guns of August 2008: Russia's War in Georgia*. Armonk: M. E. Sharpe.

Corso, M., 2009. "Georgia's Expansion Halts." *Caucasus Analytical Digest: The Caucasus in the Global Financial Crisis*, No. 6, May 21, online at http://www.hertie-school.org/binaries/addon/1282_caucasus_economic report.pdf.

Crane, K., D. J. Peterson, and O. Oliker, 2005. "Russian Investment in the Commonwealth of Independent States." *Eurasian Geography and Economics*, Vol. 46, No. 6.

Curnow, B., 2006. "Tax Administration Reform in Georgia." *Georgian Economic Trends*, June, online at http://www.geplac.ge/files/english-june.pdf.

Curtis, G. E., ed., 1995. *Armenia, Azerbaijan, and Georgia: Country Studies.* Washington, D.C.: Federal Research Division Library of Congress.

Dadalauri, N., 2008. "Political Corruption in Georgia." In *Corruption and Development: The Anti-Corruption Campaigns*, S. Bracking, ed. New York: Palgrave Macmillan.

Dadalauri, N., 2009. "Transnationalization and Georgian State: Myth or Reality?" In *The Transnationalization of States, Economies, and Civil Societies: The New Challenges for Governance in Europe*, L. Burst, and R. Holzhacker, eds. Heidelberg: Springer.

De Gregorio, J., B. Eichengreen, T. Ito, and C. Wyplosz, 1999. *An Independent and Accountable IMF.* Geneva Reports on the World Economy 1. Geneva: ICMB.

De Waal, T., 2011. *Georgia's Choices: Charting a Future in Uncertain Times*. Washington, D.C.: Carnegie Endowment, online at http://carnegieendowment.org/files/georgias_choices.pdf.

Devdariani, J., 2004. "Georgia's Rose Revolution Grapples with Dilemma: Do Ends Justify Means." *Eurasia Insight*, November 26, online at http://www.eurasianet.org/departments/insight/articles/eav102604.shtml.

Dragadze, T., 1999. "Ethnic Conflict as Political Smokescreen: The Caucasus Region." In *Ethnicity and Intra-State Conflict*, H. Wiberg, and C. P. Scherrer, eds. Aldershot: Ashgate.

Dumienski, Z., 2011. "Georgia: Singapore of the Caucasus?" *Eurasia Review. News and Analysis*, February 21, online at http://www.eurasiareview.com/analysis/georgia-singapore-of-the-caucasus-21022011/.

Ebrill L., M. Keen, J. P. Bodin, and V. Summers, 2001. *The Modern VAT*. Washington, D.C.: The IMF.

Eichengreen, B., 2000. *Can the Moral Hazard Caused by IMF Bailouts be Reduced?* Geneva: ICMB.

Eichengreen, B., 2011. Exorbitant Privilege: The Rise and Fall of the Dollar and the Future of the International Monetary System. Oxford: Oxford University Press.

EIU (Economist Intelligence Unit), 2005. "The Economist Intelligence Unit's Quality-of-Life Index." *The Economist Intelligence Unit*, online at http://www.economist.com/media/pdf/QUALITY_OF_LIFE.pdf.

EPC (Eastern Partnership Community), 2011. "Joint Declaration of the Warsaw Eastern Partnership Summit, Warsaw, 29-30 September 2011." *Eastern Partnership Community*, September 30, online at http://www.easternpartnership.org/announcement/joint-declaration-warsaw-eastern-partnership-summit-warsaw-29-30-september-2011.

ESI (European Stability Initiative), 2010. *Reinventing Georgia: The Story of a Libertarian Revolution*. Berlin – Brussels – Istanbul: European Stability Initiative, online at http://www.esiweb.org/index.php?lang=enandid=322anddebate_ID=3.

Fairbanks, C. H. Jr., 2004. "Georgia's Rose Revolution." *Journal of Democracy*, Vol. 15, Vol. 2.

Fioretos, O, 2003. "The Domestic Sources of Multilateral Preferences: Varieties of Capitalism in the European Community." In *Varieties of Capitalism: The Institutional Foundations of Comparative Advantage*, P. A. Hall, and D. Soskice, eds. New York: Oxford University Press.

Gachechiladze, R., 1995. *The New Georgia: Space, Society, Politics*. London; UCL Press.

Gaganidze, G., 2007. "Prospects of Export Orientation of the Georgian Economy." *Georgian Economic Trends*, October, online at http://www.geplac.ge/newfiles/GeorgianEconomicTrends/2007/english_october_2007.pdf.

Gegeshidze, A., 2004. "Georgia's Regional Vulnerabilities and the Ajaria Crisis." *Insight Turkey*, Vol. 6, No. 2.

Gegeshidze, A., 2009. "Georgia After the War: Toward Lasting Peace and Stability." *The Caucasus and Globalization*, Vol. 3, Iss. 1.

Gegeshidze, A., 2011. "Georgia's Political Transformation: Democracy in Zigzag." In *South Caucasus—20 Years of Independence*. Tbilisi: Friedrich-Ebert-Stiftung, online at http://www.fes.ge/images/Fes_Files/-2011_GEO/20%20years%20of%20independence%20eng.pdf.

Gegeshidze, A., and V. Papava, 2009. "Post-War Georgia Pondering New Models of Development." Central Asia-Caucasus Analyst, Vol. 11, No. 1, January 14, online at http://www.cacianalyst.org/?q=node/5012.

Giorkhelidze, D., 2010. "Social Conditions: Current Issues." *Kavkazskii Akcent*, No. 10. (In Russian.)

Giuli, M., 2009. "Georgia and the Systemic Impact of the Financial Crisis." *Caucasian Review of International Affairs*, Vo. 3(3)—Summer, online at http://www.cria-online.org/Journal/8/Done_Georgia%20and%20the%20systemic%20impact%20of%20the%20financial%20crisis_Marco%20Giuli.pdf.

Gogolashvili, K., 2007. "Convergence of the Regulatory Framework with the EU: An Important Challenge for Trade and Investment." *Georgian Economic Trends*, October, online at http://www.geplac.ge/newfiles/GeorgianEconomicTrends/2007/english_october_2007.pdf.

Gogolashvili, K., 2011. "In Search of Georgia's Economic Model." In *South Caucasus—20 Years of Independence*. Tbilisi: Friedrich-Ebert-Stiftung, online at http://www.fes.ge/images/Fes_Files/2011_GEO/20%20years%-20of%20independence%20eng.pdf.

Gomulka, S., 1995. *The IMF-Supported Programs of Poland and Russia, 1990–1994: Principles, Errors and Results*. Studies and Analyses, Working Papers, No. 36. Warsaw: CASE.

Gotsiridze, R., 2008. "National Currency of Georgia—The Lari." In *Central Eurasia: National Currencies*, E. M. Ismailov, ed. Stockholm: CAandCC Press.

Gotsiridze, R., and O. Kandelaki, 2001. "Georgia: Halfway Reforms as a Factor of the Economic Crisis." *Central Asia and the Caucasus,* No. 6.

GoG (Government of Georgia), 2003. *Economic Development and Poverty Reduction Program of Georgia.* Tbilisi.

Grigoriev, L., S. Kondratiev, and M. Salikhov, 2008. "Difficult Way out of Transformational Crisis (the Case of Georgia)." *Voprosy ekonomiki*, No. 10. (In Russian.)

Gujaraidze, N., 2010. *Aggressive Statet Property Privatization Policy on "Georgian-Style Privatization"-2*. Tbilisis: Green Alternative, OSI, online at http://www.greenalt.org/webmill/data/file/publications/privatization_report_GA_2010(1).pdf.

Gujaraidze, N., M. Barbakadze, K. Gujaraidze, R. Mchedlishvili, and K. Kakhaberi, 2007. *Aggressive Statet Property Privatization Policy on "Georgian-Style Privatization."* Tbilisis: Green Alternative, OSI, online at http://www.greenalt.org/webmill/data/file/publications/Privatizeba-Eng4.pdf.

Gularidze, T., 2003. "Russian Company Seals Controversial Takeover of Tbilisi Electricity Distribution." *Civil Georgia, Tbilisi*, August 2, online at http://www.civil.ge/eng/article.php?id=4694andsearch.

Gurgenidze, L., 2009. "Georgia's Search for Economic Liberty: A Blueprint for Reform in Developing Economies." *American Enterprise Institute for Public Policy Research, Development Policy Outlook*, No. 2., June, online at http://www.aei.org/docLib/02%20DPO%20June%202009%20newg.pdf.

Gurgenidze, L., M. Lobzhanidze, and D. Onoprishvili, 1994. "Georgia: From Planning to Hyperinflation." *Communist Economies and Economic Transformation,* Vol. 6, No. 2.

Hall, R. E., and A. Rabushka, 1995. *The Flat Tax.* Stanford: Hoover Institution Press.

Herzig, E., 1999. *The New Caucasus. Armenia, Azerbaijan and Georgia.* London: Royal Institute of International Affairs.

Hicks, R. E., W. J. Klages, and F. A. Raffa, 1971. *Economics: Myth, Method, or Madness.* Berkley: Mr. Cutchan Publishing Corporation.

Hill, F., 2004. *Energy Empire: Oil, Gas and Russia's Revival.* London, UK: The Foreign Policy Centre, online at http://www.brookings.edu/views/articles/Fhill/20040930.pdf.

HRIDC (Human Rights Information and Documentation Center), 2004. *One Step Forward, Two Steps Back. Human Rights in Georgia After the "Rose Revolution."* Tbilisi: Human Rights Information and Documentation Center, online at http://www.humanrights.ge/files/REPORT.pdf.

HRIDC (Human Rights Information and Documentation Center), 2007. *Georgia: A Flickering Beacon of Democracy. Human Rights in Georgia in 2007*. Tbilisi: Human Rights Information and Documentation Center, online at http://www.humanrights.ge/admin/editor/uploads/pdf/Annual%20Report%20HRIDC%202008.pdf.

HRIDC (Human Rights Information and Documentation Center), 2008a. *Putinization of Georgia: Georgian Media after the Rose Revolution Media in Georgia 2003-2007*. Tbilisi: Human Rights Information and Documentation Center, online at http://www.humanrights.ge/admin/editor/uploads/files/Georgian%20Media%20after%20the%20Rose%20revolution.pdf.

HRIDC (Human Rights Information and Documentation Center), 2008b. *The Big Eviction. Violations of Property Rights in Georgia*. Tbilisi: Human Rights Information and Documentation Center, online at http://www.humanrights.ge/admin/editor/uploads/files/Big%20Eviction.pdf.

Hunter, S., 1994. *The Transcaucasus in Transition: Nation-Building and Conflict*. Washington, D.C.: CSIS.

IBRD (International Bank for Reconstruction and Development), 1991. *Lessons of Tax Reform*. Washington, D.C.: The World Bank.

ICG (International Crisis Group), 2004. "Saakashvili's Ajara Success: Repeatable Elsewhere in Georgia? *Europe Briefing*," Tbilisi/Brussels, August 18, online at http://unpan1.un.org/intradoc/groups/public/documents/untc/unpan018787.pdf.

IMF (International Monetary Fund), 1991. A *Study of the Soviet Economy*. Vol. 3. Paris: OECD.

IMF (International Monetary Fund), 1997. *Reliable Governance: The Role of IMF*. Washington, D.C.: The IMF.

IMF (International Monetary Fund), 2003. "Georgia: Poverty Reduction Strategy Paper." *IMF Country Report*, No. 03/265, online at http://www.imf.org/external/pubs/ft/scr/2003/cr03265.pdf.

IMF (International Monetary Fund), 2008. *Georgia: Letter of Intent, Memorandum of Economic and Financial Policies, and Technical Memorandum of Understanding, September 9*. Washigton: The International Monetary Fund, online at http://www.imf.org/External/NP/LOI/2008/geo/090908.pdf.

Ismailov, E., and V. Papava, 2006. *The Central Caucasus: Essays on Geopolitical Economy*. Stockholm: CAandCC Press.

Ismailov, E., and V. Papava, 2008a. "A New Concept for the Caucasus." *Southeast European and Black Sea Studies*, Vo. 8, No. 3.

Ismailov, E., and V. Papava, 2008b. *The Central Caucasus: Problems of Geopolitical Economy*. New York: Nova Science Publishers.

Israelian, I., 2011. "Economy of South Caucasus: Closer to Europe?" *Kavkazskii Akcent*, No. 11. (In Russian.)

Jobelius, M., 2011a. *Economic Liberalism in Georgia: A Challenge for EU Convergence and Trade Unions*. Perspective / FES Tbilisi, April, online at http://library.fes.de/pdf-files/id/08135.pdf.

Jobelius, M., 2011b. "Georgia's Authoritarian Liberalism." In *South Caucasus—20 Years of Independence*. Tbilisi: Friedrich-Ebert-Stiftung, online at http://www.fes.ge/images/Fes_Files/2011_GEO/20%20years%-20of%20independence%20eng.pdf.

Jones, S. F., 2006. "The Rose Revolution: A Revolution without Revolutionaries?" *Cambridge Review of International Affairs*, Vol. 19, No. 1.

Jones, S. F., 2008a. "Clash in the Caucasus: Georgia, Russia, and the Fate of South Ossetia." *Origins: Current Events in Historical Perspective*, Vol. 2, Issue 2, online at http://ehistory.osu.edu/osu/origins/article.cfm?articleid=20.

Jones, S., 2008b. "Reflections on the Rose Revolution. A Tale of Two Rallies." *The Harvard International Review*, March 16, online at http://hir.harvard.edu/reflections-on-the-rose-revolution.

Jowiak, R., 2008. "EU Sets out Eastern Partnership Plans." *European Voice*, December 3, online at http://www.europeanvoice.com/Article/63276.aspx.

Kakachia, K. K., 2010. "The Russo-Georgian Relationship: Personal Issues or National Interest?" *Turkish Policy Quarterly*, Vol. 9 No. 4, online at http://www.turkishpolicy.com/dosyalar/files/Kornely%20Kakachia-%20The%20Russo-Georgian%20Relationship.pdf.

Kakulia, M., 2001. *Problems of Currency System Development in Georgia.* Tbilisi: SESPSKI. (In Georgian.)

Kakulia, M., 2007. "Labor Migrants' Remittances to Georgia: Volume, Structure and Socio-Economic Effect." *Georgian Economic Trends*, October, online at http://www.geplac.ge/newfiles/Georgian EconomicTrends/2007/english_october_2007.pdf.

Kakulia, M., 2008a. "Before and After the Introduction of the Lari: Georgian National Currency in Retrospect." In E. M. Ismailov, ed. *Central Eurasia: National Currencies*. Stockholm: CAandCC Press.

Kakulia, M., 2008b. "Mitigating Post-War Economic Threats in Georgia." *Georgian Economic Trends*, October, online at http://www.geplac.ge/newfiles/GeorgianEconomicTrends/2008/October%202008%20(eng).pdf.

Kakulia, M., 2011. "Economic Integration and Regulatory Convergence with the EU Polices: A View from Georgia." In *Eastern Partnership for the South Caucasus*, I. Lomitashvili, and A. Watt, eds. Tbilisi: Levan

Mikeladze Foundation, online at http://www.fes.ge/images/Fes_Files/2011_GEO/miqelazis%20fondis%20jurnali%20ing.pdf.

Kakulia, M., and N. Gigineishvili, 2005. "The Primary Objectives and Priorities of Monetary Policy in Georgia." *Problems of Economic Transition*, Vol. 48, No. 4.

Kalicki, J. H., 2001. "Caspian Energy at the Crossroads." *Foreign Affairs*, Vol. 80, No. 5.

Kaminski, B., 1996. "Factors Affecting Trade Reorientation of the Newly Independent States." In *Economic Transition in Russia and the New States of Eurasia*, B. Kaminski, ed. Armonk: M. E. Sharpe.

Karumidze, Z., and J. V. Wertsch, eds., 2005. *"Enough." The Rose Revolution in the Republic of Georgia 2003*. New York: Nova Science Publishers.

Kellogg, A., 2011. "Israeli Businessmen on Trial in Tbilisi." *FOX News*, January 18, online at http://liveshots.blogs.foxnews.com/2011/01/18/israeli-businessmen-on-trial-in-tbilisi/.

Kemkhadze, S., 2007. "Inconsistencies in Georgia's Food Safety System Reform and Ways Forward." *Georgian Economic Trends*, July, online at http://www.geplac.ge/newfiles/GeorgianEconomicTrends/2007/english-july%201.pdf.

Khaduri, N., 2005a. "Macroeconomic Determinants of Competitiveness of the Georgian Economy." *Georgian Economic Trends*, No. 3, December, online at http://www.geplac.ge/files/10150_9_706303_ec_trends_dec2005_en.pdf.

Khaduri, N., 2005b. "Mistakes Made in Conducting Economic Reforms in Postcommunist Georgia." *Problems of Economic Transition*, Vol. 48, No. 4.

Khaduri, N., 2006. "Georgian Economy." In *Central Eurazia 2005. Analytical Annual*. Luleå: CAandCC Press.

Khaduri, N., 2009. "Georgia: Economy." In *Central Eurasia 2008. Analytical Annual*. Luleå: CAandCC Press.

Khaduri, N., 2010a. "Economic System in Georgia." In *Moving Closer to Europe? Economic and Social Polices in Georgia, Armenia and Azerbaijan*. Tbilisi: Centre for Economic Problems Research, Friedrich-Ebert-Stiftung, online at http://cepr.ge/images/doc/CEPR%20FES%20Book%20ENG.pdf .

Khaduri, N., 2010b. "The Central Caucasus—Reforms and the Road to Europe." *The Caucasus and Globalization*, Vol. 4, Iss. 3-4.

Khechinashvili, D., 2005. "Georgia After the Rose Revolution: An Opportunity Lost?," *Economic Reform, Feature Service*, Center for

International Private Enterprise, October 31, online at http://www.cipe.org/pdf/publications/fs/103105.pdf.

Khelashvili, G., 2011. *Georgia's Foreign Policy Impasse. Is Consensus Crumbling?* PONARS Eurasia Policy Memo No. 187, September, online at http://www.gwu.edu/~ieresgwu/assets/docs/ponars/pepm_187.pdf.

Khidasheli, T., 2011a. "Democracy and Good Governance within the EAP Context: A View from Georgia." In *Eastern Partnership for the South Caucasus*, I. Lomitashvili, and A. Watt, eds. Tbilisi: Levan Mikeladze Foundation, online at http://www.fes.ge/images/ Fes_Files/2011_GEO/miqelazis%20fondis%20jurnali%20ing.pdf.

Khidasheli, T., 2011b. "Georgia and Eastern Partnership—Problems and Challenges in Terms of Protection of Human Rights." In *Opinions on Georgia's European Future*, G. Magularia, ed. Tbilisi: Levan Mikeladze Foundation.

Khutsidze, N., 2003. "Adjara Hopes to Get a Special Economic Zone." *Civil.Ge, Daily News Online*, March 27, online at http://www.civil.ge/eng/article.php?id=3413andsearch=papava.

Khutsidze, N., 2004. "QandA with Legal Expert Davit Usupashvili." *Civil.Ge, Daily News Online*, November 1, online at http://www.civil.ge/eng/article.php?id=8231.

Khutsidze, N., 2007. "MP Speaks Out Against Free Economic Zone." *Civil.Ge, Daily News Online*, May 18, online at http://www.civil.ge/eng/article.php?id=15143andsearch=papava.

Khutsishvili, G., ed., 2008. *Civil Society and Rose Revolution in Georgia*. Tbilisi: ICCN–Cordaid.

King, C., 2004. "A Rose Among Thorns." *Foreign Affairs*, Vol. 83, Iss. 2.

King, C., 2008. "The Five-Day War. Managing Moscow After the Georgia Crisis." *Foreign Affairs*, Vol. 87, No. 6, November/December.

Kissinger, H., 2002. *Does America Need a Foreign Policy? Toward a Diplomacy for the Twenty-First Century*. London: The Free Press.

Koberidze, L., 2009. "Why it is Impossible to Bankrupt Already Bankrupt Entities." *BusinessPresa.ge*, November 27, online at http://anonymouse.ru:8080/newmouse/browse.php?u=Oi8vYnVzaW5lc3 MucHJlc2EuZ2UvP3A9MjU3Ng%3D%3Dandb=5. (In Georgian.)

Krugman, P., 2008. *The Return of Depression Economics and the Crisis of 2008*. New York: Norton.

Kupatadze, A., 2007. "Political-Criminal-Business Nexus in Georgia and Kyrgyzstan Comparative analysis." *Research Fellows New*, Bishkek: Social Research Centre, American University of Central Asia, online at http://src.auca.kg/images/stories/files/Report_Aleko_Kupatadze_eng_19June.pdf.

Kupchan, C. A., 2006. "Wilted Rose. Sukhumi Dispatch." *The New Republic*, Vol. 234; Iss. 4751, February 6.

Kutivadze, N., 2011. "Georgian Government's New Legislative Initiative—Universal Competition Agency Without Sector Regulator?" *Transparency International Georgia*, September 28, online at http://www.transparency.ge/en/blog/pgeorgian-government%E2%80%99s-new-legislative-initiative%E2%80%93-universal-competition-agency-without-sector-.

Lang, D. M., 1966. *The Georgians*. New York: Praeger.

Lanskoy, M., and G. Areshidze, 2008. "Georgia's Year of Turmoil." *Journal of Democracy*, Vol. 19, No. 4.

Lavigne, M., 1995. *The Economics of Transition. From Socialist Economy to Market Economy.* New York: St. Martin's Press.

Lashkhi, I., N. Evgenidze, D. Narmania, and M., Gabedava, 2008. *The "50-Day Program" of the Government of Georgia: Analysis and Conclusions.* Open Society Georgia Foundation Policy Paper No. 15. Tbilisi: OSGF.

Lazarus, J., 2010. *Neo-Liberal State Building and Western 'Democracy Promotion:' the Case of Georgia*. Prepared for delivery at the 2010 SGIR 7th Pan-European Conference on International Relations, Stockholm, Sweden, September 9-11, 2010, online at http://stockholm.sgir.eu/uploads/Neo-liberal%20state%20building%20and%20democracy%20promotion%20in%20Georgia.pdf.

Leiashvili, P., 2010. "Algorithms of Democratization in a Totalitarian Society (A Case Study Of Georgia)." *The Caucasus and Globalization*, Vol. 4, Iss. 1-2.

Levitsky, S., and L. A. Way, 2010. *Competitive Authoritarianism: Hybrid Regimes After the Cold War (Problems of International Politics).* New York: Cambridge University Press.

Liloyan, T., 2004. "Armsberbank to Become Russian Vneshtorgbank Subsidiary." *Armenian Diaspora.com*, March 24, online at http://www.armeniandiaspora.com/showthread.php?795-Armsberbank-to-become-Russian-Vneshtorgbank-subsidiary.

MacFarlane, S. N., 2011. Post-Revolutionary Georgia on the Edge? *Chatham House Briefing Paper, March 2011, online at http://www.chathamhouse.org/sites/default/files/public/Research/Russia%20and%20Eurasia/bp0311_macfarlane.pdf.*

Maisaia, V., 2007. *The Caucasus-Caspian Regional and Energy Security Agendas—Past, Contemporary and Future Geopolitics: View from Georgia*. Brussels–Tbilisi: Tbiliselebi.

Maksoeva, V., 2010. "Not Singapore, but Cyprus!" *Kavkazskii Akcent*, No. 10. (In Russian.)

MCC (Millennium Challenge Corporation), 2005. "Millennium Challenge Corporation Board Approves $295.3 Million Compact with Georgia." *Millennium Challenge Corporation*, August 16, online at http://www.mcc.gov/pages/press/release/release-081605-mccboardapproves.

McDonald, M., 2005. "Democracy Flourishes a Year After Georgia's Rose Revolution." *HighBeam Business*, March 8, online at http://business.highbeam.com/435343/article-1G1-130186618/democracy-flourishes-year-after-georgia-rose-revolution.

Mekantsishvili, E., 2009. "Macroeconomic Analysis of Georgia's Economic Development using a Social Accounting Matrix (1999-2008)." *The Caucasus and Globalization*, Vol. 3, Iss. 4.

Mekvabishvili, E., 2009. *Globalization of Economy: Directions, Challenges, Perspectives*. Tbilisi: Inovatsia. (In Georgian.)

Meskhia, I., 2008. "Living Standards and Poverty in Georgia." *Georgian Economic Trends*, May, online at http://www.geplac.ge/newfiles/GeorgianEconomicTrends/2008/May%202008%20engl.pdf.

Metreveli, R., 1995. *Georgia*. Nashville: Publisher's International.

Milanovic, B., 1998. *Income, Inequality and Poverty during the Transition from Planned to Market Economy*. Washington, D.C: The World Bank.

Milcher, S., and B. Slay, 2005. *The Economics of the 'European Neighbourhood Policy:' An initial Assessment*. Studies and Analyses, Working Papers, No. 291. Warsaw: CASE, online at http://www.case.com.pl/upload/publikacja_plik/4932826_SA%20291accepted.pdf.

Miller, E., 2004. "Smelling the Roses: Eduard Shevardnadze's End and Georgia's Future." *Problems of Post-Communism*, Vol. 51, No. 2.

Mishan, E. J., 1986. *Economic Myths and the Mythology of Economics*. Atlantic Highlands: Humanities Press International.

Mitchell, L. A., 2006. "Democracy on Georgia Since the Rose Revolution." *Orbis. A Journal of World Affairs*, Vol. 50, No. 4, pp. 669-676.

Mitchell, L. A., 2007. "Beacon of Democracy or Khachapuri Republic?" *The National Interest*, December 13, online at http://nationalinterest.org/

commentary/inside-track-beacon-of-democracy-or-khachapuri-republic-1905.

Mitchell, L., 2008. "What was the Rose Revolution For? Understanding the Georgian Revolution." *The Harvard International Review*, February 27, online at http://hir.harvard.edu/what-was-the-rose-revolution-for.

Mitchell, L. A, 2009. *Uncertain Democracy: U.S. Foreign Policy and Georgia's Rose Revolution*. Philadelphia: University of Pennsylvania Press.

Mitchell, L. A., 2010. "Georgia's Paradoxes." *The Faster Times*, November 9, online at http://thefastertimes.com/foreignpolicy/2010/11/09/georgias-paradoxes/.

Mkrtchyan, T., T. Huseynov, and K. Gogolashvili, 2009. *The European Union and the South Caucasus. Three Perspectives on the Future of the European Project from the Caucasus. Europe in Dialogue 2009/01*. Gütersloh: Bertelsmann Stiftung.

Muskhelishvili, M., 2010. "Georgia in a New Wave of Transformation." *The Caucasus and Globalization*, Vol. 4, Iss. 1-2.

Nafziger, E. W., 1997. *The Economics of Developing Countries*. Upper Saddle River: Prentice Hall.

Narmania, D., 2009. "Economic Policy in Georgia: Liberalization, Economic Crises and Changes." *Turkish Policy Quarterly*, Vol. 8, No. 2, online at http://www.ciesr.org/uploads/publications/tpq_davitnarmania.pdf.

Natelauri, I., 2007. "Georgia's External Sector: Current State and Problems." *The Caucasus and Globalization*, Vol. 1 (4).

Natelauri, I., 2009. "Microeconomic Environment in Post-Soviet Georgia: Reverses and Paradoxes." *The Caucasus and Globalization*, Vol. 3, Iss. 1.

Natelauri, I., 2010. "Employment Problems and Short-Term Economic Benefits in Post-Communist Countries (Georgian Case Study)." *The Caucasus and Globalization*, Vol. 4, Iss. 1-2.

NBG (National Bank of Georgia), 2011. "Workers' Remittances by Major Partner Countries." *Money Transfers by Countries, National Bank of Georgia*, online at http://www.nbg.gov.ge/uploads/moneytransfers/money_transfers_by_countrieseng.xls.

Nodia, G., 2000. "A New Cycle of Instability in Georgia. New Troubles and Old Problems." In *Crossroads and Conflict: Security and Foreign Policy in the Caucasus and Central Asia*, G. K. Bertsch, C. Craft, S. A. Jones, and M. Beck, eds. New York: Routledge.

Nodia, G., 2005. "The Dynamics and Sustainability of the Rose Revolution." In *Democratisation in the European Neighbourhood*, M. Emerson, ed.

Brussels: Centre for European Policy Studies, online at http://www.uquebec.ca/observgo/fichiers/57785_1267.pdf.

NSOG (National Statistics Office of Georgia), 2011a. "CPI (Inflation)." *The National Statistics Office of Georgia*, online at http://www.geostat.ge /index.php?action=pageandp_id=128andlang=eng.

NSOG (National Statistics Office of Georgia), 2011b. "External Trade of Georgia by Countries." *The National Statistics Office of Georgia*, online at http://www.geostat.ge/index.php?action=pageandp_id=137andlang=eng.

NSOG (National Statistics Office of Georgia), 2011c. "Gross Domestic Product (GDP)." *The National Statistics Office of Georgia*, online at http://www.geostat.ge/index.php?action=pageandp_id=119andlang=eng.

O'Ballance, E., 1997. *Wars in the Caucasus, 1990-1995.*, New York: New York University Press.

OSCE (Organization for Security and Co-operation in Europe), 2008a. *Georgia. Extraordinary Presidential Election, 5 January 2008. PSCE/ODIHR Election Observation Mission Final Report, March 4 2008.* Warsaw: OSCE, online at http://www.osce.org/odihr/ elections/georgia/30959.

OSCE (Organization for Security and Co-operation in Europe), 2008b. *Statement of Parliamentary Findings and Conclusions. International Election Observation Mission. Georgia—Parliament Elections, May 21 2008.* Tbilisi: OSCE, online at http://www.osce.org/odihr/ elections/georgia/32017.

Papaphilippou, A., 2008. "Risks for the Sustainability of Georgia's Economic Growth." *Georgian Economic Trends*, February, online at http://www.geplac.ge/newfiles/GeorgianEconomicTrends/2008/February %202008%20eng.pdf.

Papava, V., 1990. "On the Concepts of Economic Reform in the USSR." *Ekonomika i matamaticheskie metody,* Vol. 26, No. 6. (In Russian).

Papava, V., 1992. "Privatization of Major Production Factors." *Fair Play, Problems of Management,* No. 3. (In Russian).

Papava, V., 1995a. "The Georgian Economy: Problems of Reform." *Eurasian Studies* Vol. 2, No. 2.

Papava, V., 1995b. "Marxist Points of View on the Soviet Communist Economic System and the Manifestation of Egalitarianism in Post-Communist Economic Reform." *International Journal of Social Economics,* Vol. 22, No. 6.

Papava, V., 1996a. "The Georgian Economy: From "Shock Therapy" to "Social Promotion"." *Communist Economies and Economic Transformation,* Vol. 8, No. 8.

Papava, V., 1996b. "'Social Promotion' of Economic Reform in Georgia." *Economic Systems,* Vol. 20, No.4.

Papava, V., 1998. "Toward the Progress of Reform and Prospects of Economic Growth." *Obscestvo i ekonomika,* No. 2. (In Russian.)

Papava, V., 1999. "The Georgian Economy: Main Directions and Initial Results of Reforms." In *Systemic Change in Post-Communist Economies,* P. G. Hare, ed. London: Macmillan Press.

Papava, V., 2000a. "Economic Approach to the Restriction of Corruption in Georgia." *Georgian Economic Trends,* No. 3-4, online at http://www.geplac.ge/publicat/economic/archives/get00n3n4e.pdf.

Papava, V., 2000b. "On the Theory of Post-Communist Transformation of Economy." *Obschestvo i ekonomika,* No. 7. (In Russian).

Papava V., 2001. Necroeconomics—A Phenomenon of the Post-Communist Transition Period. *Problems of Economic Transition,* Vol. 44, No. 8.

Papava, V., 2002a. *Leszek Balcerowicz and Georgia.* Tbilisi: GFSIS.

Papava, V., 2002b. Necroeconomics—the Theory of Post-Communist Transformation of an Economy. *International Journal of Social Economics,* Vol. 29, No. 9/10.

Papava, V., 2003a. *Splendours and Miseries of the IMF in Post-Communist Georgia.* Laredo: We-publish.com.

Papava V., 2003b. "On the Role of the International Monetary Fund in the Post-Communist Transformation of Georgia." *Emerging Markets Finance and Trade,* 2003, Vol. 39, No. 5.

Papava, V., 2005a. "Georgia's Macroeconomic Situation Before and After the Rose Revolution." *Problems of Economic Transition*, Vol. 48, No. 4.

Papava, V., 2005b. "Georgia's Economic Role in the South Caucasus." *Problems of Economic Transition*, Vol. 48, No. 4.

Papava, V., 2005c. *Necroecononics: The Political Economy of Post-Communist Capitalism (Lessons from Georgia).* New York: iUniverse.

Papava, V., 2005d. "On the Theory of Post-Communist Economic Transition to Market." *International Journal of Social Economics,* Vol. 32, No. 1/2.

Papava, V., 2005e. "The Baku–Tbilisi–Ceyhan Pipeline: Implications for Georgia." In *The Baku–Tbilisi–Ceyhan Pipeline: Oil Window to the West,* S. F. Starr, and S. E. Cornell, eds. Washington, D.C., Uppsala: Johns Hopkins University-SAIS, Uppsala University, online at www.silkroadstudies.org/BTC_5.pdf.

Papava, V., 2006a. "Comparative Advantages of the Central Caucasian Countries: Potential, Realised, and Missed Opportunities." *The Caucasus and Globalisation*, No. 1.

Papava, V., 2006b. "Corruption and Primary Accumulation of Capital in Transitional Economies." *Ludwig von Mises Institute Working Papers*, 10/17/2006, online at http://www.mises.org/journals/scholar/papava.pdf.

Papava, V., 2006c. "The Political Economy of Georgia's Rose Revolution." *Orbis. A Journal of World Affairs*, Vol. 50, No. 4, pp. 657-667.

Papava, V., 2007a. "Currency Board Against the Background of Dutch Disease." *Georgian Economic Trends*, October, online at http://www.geplac.ge/newfiles/GeorgianEconomicTrends/2007/english_october_2007.pdf.

Papava, V., 2007b. "Russia's Illiberal 'Liberal Empire'." *Project Syndicate*, February 28, online at http://www.project-syndicate.org/commentary/papava2.

Papava, V., 2007c. *The "Immortal" Idea of a Free Economic Zone*. Georgian Foundation for Strategic and International Studies Expert Opinion, No 2. Tbilisi: GFSIS, online at http://www.gfsis.org/media/download/library/articles/EXPERT_OPINION_VLADIMER_PAPAVA_ENG.pdf.

Papava, V., 2008a. "Can Georgia Avoid a Currency Crisis?" *Georgian Business Week*, December 15, online at http://www.gbw.ge/news.aspx?sid=f5538a24-650f-4375-bf36-618a266d1079.

Papava, V., 2008b. "Georgia's Green Friday." *The Georgian Times*, November 17, online at http://www.geotimes.ge/index.php?m=homeandnewsid=13663.

Papava, V., 2008c. "Georgia's Hollow Revolution. Does Georgia's Pro-Western and Anti-Russian Policy Amount to Democracy?" *The Harvard International Review*, February 27, online at http://hir.harvard.edu/georgia-s-hollow-revolution.

Papava, V., 2008d. "Is Georgians' European Dream Any Part of Government Policy?" *The Georgian Times*, December 15, online at http://www.geotimes.ge/index.php?m=homeandnewsid=14166.

Papava, V., 2008e. "On the Role of the "Caucasian Tandem" in GUAM." *Central Asia and the Caucasus*, No. 3-4 (51-52).

Papava, V., 2008f. "Post-War Georgia's Economic Challenges." *Central Asia-Caucasus Analyst*, Vol. 10, No. 23, November 26, online at http://www.cacianalyst.org/?q=node/4991.

Papava, V., 2008g. "The Essence of Economic Reforms in Post-Revolution Georgia: What about the European Choice?" *Georgian International Journal of Science and Technology*, Vol. 1, Issue 1.

Papava, V., 2009a. "Anatomical Pathology of Georgia's Rose Revolution." *Current Politics and Economics of the Caucasus Region*, Vol. 2, Issue 1.

Papava, V., 2009b. "Georgian Economy: Mistakes, Threats and Resolutions." In *Crisis in Georgia, 2008: Preconditions, Reality, Perspectives*, S. Tsiskarishvili, ed. Tbilisi: Independent Experts' Club, online at http://www.fes.ge/images/Fes_Files/09_GeoP/crisis%202008%20in%20georgia_final.pdf.

Papava, V., 2009c. "Georgia's Economy: Post-Revolutionary Development and Post-War Difficulties." *Central Asian Survey*, Vol. 28, No. 2.

Papava, V., 2009d. "Post-war Georgia: Current Developments and Challenges Ahead." *Policy Brief ISPI*, No. 127—April, online at http://www.ispionline.it/it/documents/PB_127_2009.pdf.

Papava, V., 2009e. "Poverty Reduction Through Private Sector Development in Georgia: Policy, Practice and Perspectives." *Caucasian Review of International Affairs*, Vol. 3 (3)—Summer, online at http://www.cria-online.org/Journal/8/Done_Poverty%20reduction%20through%20private%20sector%20development%20in%20Georgia_Vladimer%20Papava.pdf.

Papava, V., 2009f. "The European Vector of Economic Reforms in Post-Revolution Georgia." In *Georgia in Transition*, L. King, and G. Khubua, eds. Frankfurt am Main: Peter Lang.

Papava, V., 2009g. "The "Rosy" Mistakes of the IMF and World Bank in Georgia." *Problems of Economic Transition*, Vol. 52, No. 7.

Papava, V., 2010a. "Economy of the Post-Communist Capitalism under the Financial Crisis." *Studies in Economics and Finance*, Vol. 27, No. 2.

Papava, V., 2010b. "Georgia's Economy: Post-Revolutionary Development and Post-War Difficulties." In *War and Revolution in the Caucasus: Georgia Ablaze*, S. F. Jones, ed. London: Routledge.

Papava, V., 2010c. "Post-Soviet Economic Relations between Georgia and Russia: Reality and Development Potential." In *Russia and Georgia: The Ways out of the Crisis*, G. Khutsishvili, and T. Gogueliani. Tbilisi: ICCN, online at http://www.iccn.ge/text/eng/publications/2011/Russia-Georgia-eng.pdf.

Papava, V., 2010d. "Post-War Economy of Georgia: New Challenges and Old Mistakes." In Georgia, 2009. *Post-War Challenges and Perspectives*, S. Tsiskarishvili, ed. Tbilisi: Independent Experts' Club, online at http://www.fes.ge/images/Fes_Files/2010-GEO/ieclub.2009%20eng.web.pdf.

Papava, V., 2010e. *The Economic Development Complex in the Black Sea Area: The Impact of the Global Financial and Economic Crisis.* Xenophon Paper, No. 9. Athens: ICBSS, online at http://icbss.org/images/papers/xenophon_paper_no9.pdf.

Papava, V., 2010f. “The Economic Challenges of the Black Sea Region: the Global Financial Crisis and Energy Sector Cooperation.” *Southeast European and Black Sea Studies*, Vo. 10, No. 3.

Papava, V., 2010g. “The Problem of Zombification of the Postcommunist Necroeconomy.” *Problems of Economic Transition*, Vol. 53, No. 4.

Papava, V., 2011a. “Arménie, Azerbaïdjan, Géorgie: vingt ans de transition économique.” *Les Cahiers de L'Orient*, No. 101.

Papava, V., 2011b. “Economic Achievements in Post-Revolutionary Georgia: Myths and Reality.” *Vestnik instituta Kennana v Rossii*, Iss. 19. (In Russian.)

Papava, V., 2011c. “Economic Transformation and the Impacts of the Global Financial Crisis in the Southern Caucasus.” In *Non-Traditional Security Threats and Regional Cooperation in the Southern Caucasus*, M. Aydin, ed. Amsterdam: IOS Press BV.

Papava, V., and T. Beridze, 1994. “Problems of Reforming of Georgian Economy.” *Rossiiskii ekonomicheskii zhurnal*, № 3. (In Russian).

Papava, V., and T. Beridze, 1996/1997. “Industrial Policy and Trade Regime in Georgia.” *Eurasian Studies,* Vol., 3, No. 4.

Papava, V., and E. Chikovani, eds., 1997. “Georgia: Economic and Social Challenges of the Transition.” *Problems of Economic Transition*, Vol. 40, No. 7/8.

Papava, V., and V. Chocheli, 2003. *Financial Globalization and Post-Communist Georgia. Global Exchange Rate Instability and its Implications for Georgia.* New York: iUniverse.

Papava, V., and F. Starr, 2006. “Russia’s Economic Imperialism.” *Project Syndicate*, January 17, online at http://www.project-syndicate.org/commentary/papava1.

Papava, V., and M. Tokmazishvili, 2006. “Becoming European. Georgia’s Strategy for Joining the EU.” *Problems of Post-Communism*, Vo. 53, No. 1.

Papava, V., and M. Tokmazishvili, 2007. “Necroeconomic Foundations and the Development of Business in Post-Revolution Georgia.” *The Caucasus and Globalization,* Vol. 1 (3).

Parsons, R., 2006. “Russia/Georgia: Russia Impounds Georgian Mineral Water.” *Radio Free Europe/Radio Liberty*, April 19, online at http://www.rferl.org/featuresarticle/2006/04/e3ee1b53-6b14-4553-a05d-4aa389364dd0.html.

Patsuria, N., 2008. “Port Power: Georgia Hopes Poti will Fuel Country’s Economic Recovery.”*Eurasia Insight. Eurasianet*, April 3, online at http://www.eurasianet.org/departments/insight/articles/eav040308aa.shtml.

Patsuria, N., 2011. “Georgian Electricity System Russianized.” *Georgian Journal*, April 20, online at http://georgianjournal.ge/index.php?option=com_contentandview=articleandid=4892:georgian-electricity-system-russianizedandcatid=4:economyandItemid=6.

Perovič, J., 2005. “From Disengagement to Active Economic Competition: Russia’s Return to the South Caucasus and Central Asia.” *Demokratizatsiya*, Vol. 13, No. 1, online at http://www.demokratizatsiya.org/bin/pdf/DEM%2013-1%20Perovic.pdf.

Phillips, D. L., 2004. *Stability, Security, and Sovereignty in the Republic of Georgia.* New York: The Council on Foreign Relations.

Popjanevski, J., 2011. *International Law and the Post-2008 Status Quo in Georgia: Implications for Western Policies*. Silk Road Paper, May, Washington, D.C.: Central Asia-Caucasus Institute and Silk Road Studies Program—A Joint Transatlantic Research and Policy Center, online at http://www.isdp.eu/images/stories/isdp-main-pdf/2011_popjanevski_international-law-and-the-post-2008-status-quo.pdf.

Radon, J., and D. Onoprishvili, 2003. “Rescuing Georgia.” *Project Syndicate*. December 29, online at http://www.project-syndicate.org/commentary radon1/English.

Rondeli, A., 2001. “The Choice of Independent Georgia.” In *The Security of the Caspian Sea Region*, G. Chufrin, ed. New York: Oxford University Press.

Roubanis, I. 2009. “Georgia’s Pluralistic Feudalism: A Frontline Report.” *open Democracy*, July 3, online at http://www.opendemocracy.net/article/georgia-pluralistic-feudalism#.

Rukhadze, I., and M. Hauf, 2009. “The Georgian Economy Under Saakashvili.” *The Financial*, April 21, online at http://www.finchannel.com/index.php?option=com_contentandtask=viewandid=35088andItemid=13.

Sakevarishvili, R., 2010. "Georgia: Continued Reverberations of the Crisis." *Caucasus Analytical Digest*, No. 18, July 5, online at http://georgien.boell-net.de/downloads/CaucasusAnalyticalDigest18(1).pdf.

Sakevarishvili, R., 2011. "Approximation to the EU Principles on Competition and Antimonopoly Regulations in Georgia." In *Opinions on Georgia's European Future*, G. Magularia, ed. Tbilisi: Levan Mikeladze Foundation.

Salieva, D., and A. Matayev, 2007. "Kazakh Invests in Georgian Market." *Brosse Street Journal*, May 30, online at http://www.bsj.ge/backend/viewnews.cgi?id=EElEyFklZAYyGwtrwHandstyle=printandtmpl=printnews.

Samson, I., 2006. "The Search for a Development Path: Challenges for Georgia." *Georgian Economic Trends*, No. 4, March, online at http://www.geplac.ge/files/georgian_2006_4.pdf.

Samson, I., 2008. "Medium-Term Prospects for the Georgian Economy." *Georgian Economic Trends*, February, online at http://www.geplac.ge/newfiles/GeorgianEconomicTrends/2008/February%202008%20eng.pdf.

Schaffer, M., 1992. *The Economy of Poland*. Center for Economic Performance, Discussion Paper, No. 67. London: LSE.

Schneider, F., A. Buehn, and C. E. Montenegro, 2010. *Shadow Economies All over the World: New Estimates for 162 Countries from 1999 to 2007*. The World Bank Development Research Group Policy Research Working Paper No. 5356, online at http://www-wds.worldbank.org/external/default/WDSContentServer/IW3P/IB/2010/10/14/000158349_20101014160704/Rendered/PDF/WPS5356.pdf.

Sekarev, A., 2010. "European Integration Process of Georgia, the Republic of Armenia and the Republic of Azerbaijan: Achievements, Shortcomings, Challenges." In *Moving Closer to Europe? Economic and Social Polices in Georgia, Armenia and Azerbaijan*. Tbilisi: Centre for Economic Problems Research, Friedrich-Ebert-Stiftung, online at http://cepr.ge/images/doc/CEPR%20FES%20Book%20ENG.pdf .

Shevardnadze, E., 1999. *Great Silk Route. TRACECA-PETrA. Transport Corridor Europe-Caucasus-Asia. The Eurasian Common Market. Political and Economic Aspects*. Tbilisi: Georgian Transport System.

Shmidt, M., 2007. "Foreign Direct Investment to Georgia: Can Active Investment Promotion Polices Make a Difference?" *Georgian Economic Trends*, January, online at http://www.geplac.ge/newfiles/GeorgianEconomicTrends/2007/english--january_2007.pdf.

Shome, P. ed., 1995. *Tax Policy Handbook*. Washington, D.C.: The IMF.

Shveits, M., 2011. "Lukashenko Dreams about Singapore." *Rosbalt*, January 5, online at http://www.rosbalt.ru/main/2011/01/05/806809.html. (In Russian.)

Silagadze, A., 2010. "Current Financial and Monetary Trends in Georgia." *The Caucasus and Globalization*, Vol. 4, Iss. 1-2.

Silagadze, A., and T. Atanelashvili, 2010. *Modern State Finances of Georgia*. Palo Alto: Academy Press.

Silagadze, A., and T. Beridze, 1996. "Note on Privatization in Georgia." In *Economic Transition in Russia and the New States of Eurasia*, B. Kamiński, ed. New York, M. E. Sharpe, 1996.

Silagadze, A., and S. Gelashvili, 2009. *Gegenwärtige Finanz-und Monetäre Aspekte in Georgien*. Finanzwissenschaftliche Diskussionsbeiträge Special Series, No. G-10. Potsdam: Universität Potsdam.

Silagadze, A., and M. Tokmazishvili, 2009. *Challenges of the Post-Communist Financial-Currency Policy*. New York: Nova Science Publishers.

Simons, Jr., T. W., 2008. *Eurasia's New Frontiers: Young States, Old Societies, Open Futures*. Ithaca: Cornell University Press.

Slemrod J., and J. Bakija, 1996. *Taxing Ourselves: A Citizen's Guide to the Great Debate over Tax Reform.* Cambridge: MIT Press.

Slider, D., 1995. "Georgia." In *Armenia, Azerbaijan, and Georgia: Country Studies*, G. E. Curtis, ed. Washington, D.C.: Federal Research Division Library of Congress.

Smith, K. C., 2004. *Russian Energy Politics in the Baltics, Poland, and Ukraine. A New Stealth Imperialism?* Washington, D.C.: The CSIS Press.

Socor, V., 2006. "Gazprom's 'Pure Commerce' in Georgia." *Eurasia Daily Monitor, The Jamestown Foundation*, Vol. 3, Issue 208, November 9, online at http://www.jamestown.org/single/?no_cache=1andtx_ttnews%5Btt_news%5D=32215.

SRI (Strategic Research Institute), 2003. *Lost Potential in the South Caucasus: Aspects of Interstate Trade.* Yerevan: ANTARES, 2003.

Starr, S. F., and S. E. Cornell, 2005. "The Politics of Pipelines: Bringing Caspian Energy to Markets." *SAISPHERE.*

Stiglitz, J. E., 1996. *Whither Socialism?* Cambridge: The MIT Press.

Stiglitz, J. E., 1999. "The World Bank at the Millennium." *Economic Journal,* Vol. 109, No. 459.

Stiglitz, J. E., 2010. *Freefall: America, Free Markets, and the Sinking of the World Economy*. New York: W. W. Norton and Company.

Subacchi, P., and A. Monsarrat, 2009. *New Ideas for the London Summit. Recommendations to the G20 Leaders*. London: The Royal Institute of International Affairs, Chatham House.

Subari, S., 2007. *The Anatomy of Human Rights Violations in Georgia. Human Rights in Georgia. Report of the Public Defender of Georgia*. Tbilisi: Public Defender of Georgia.

Suny, R. G., 1994. *The Making of the Georgian Nation.* Bloomington: Indiana University Press.

Tanzi, V., 1992. "Fiscal Restructuring and the Tax System." In *Structural Adjustment and Macroeconomic Policy Issues*, V. A. Jafarey, ed. Washington, D.C.: The IMF.

Tanzi, V., ed., 1993. *Fiscal Policies in Economies in Transition.* Washington, D.C.: The IMF.

Tanzi, V. ed., 1994. *Transition to Market: Studies in Fiscal Reform.* Washington, D.C.: The IMF.

Tokmazishvili, M., and J. Archvadze, 2007. "Socio–Economic and Institutional Aspects of Labor Market Development in Georgia." *Georgian Economic Trends*, July, online at http://www.geplac.ge/newfiles/GeorgianEconomicTrends/2007/english-july%201.pdf.

Tokmazishvili, M., and A. Silagadze, 2008. "The Central Caucasian Countries: Trends in Foreign Trade Relations." *The Caucasus and Globalization*, Vol. 2, Iss. 4.

Torbakov, I., 2003. "Russian Policymakers Air Notion of 'Liberal Empire' in Caucasus, Central Asia." *Eurasia Insight. Eurasianet*, October 27, online at http://www.eurasianet.org/departments/insight/articles/eav102703.shtml.

Trenin, D., 2005. *Reading Russia Right.* Carnegie Endowment for International Peace Policy Brief No. 42, October. Washington, D.C.: Carnegie Endowment for International Peace.

Truman, E. M., 2006. *A Strategy for IMF Reform.* Washington, D.C.: IIE.

Truman, E. M., ed., 2006. *Reforming the IMF for the 21st Century.* Washington, D.C.: IIE.

Tsereteli, M., 2004. "The Political Economy of the Ajarian Crisis." *Central Asia-Caucasus Analyst.* Central Asia- Caucasus Institute, April 21, online at http://www.cacianalyst.org/?q=node/2037.

Tsereteli, M., 2006. "Banned in Russia: The Politics of Georgian Wine." *Central Asia-Caucasus Analyst*, April 19, online at http://www.cacianalyst.org/?q=node/3904.

Tsiskarishvili, S., ed., 2009. *Crisis in Georgia, 2008: Preconditions, Reality, Perspectives.* Tbilisi: Independent Experts' Club, online at http://www.fes.ge/images/Fes_Files/09_GeoP/crisis%202008%20in%20georgia_final.pdf.

Tsiskarishvili, S., ed., 2010. *Georgia, 2009: Post-War Challenges and Perspectives.* Tbilisi: Independent Experts' Club, online at http://www.fes.ge/images/Fes_Files/2010-GEO/ieclub.2009%20eng.web.pdf.

Tvalchrelidze, A., A. Silagadze, G. Keshelashvili, and D. Gegia, 2011. *Georgia's Social and Economic Development Program.* Tbilisi: International Foundation for Sustainable Development—Georgia, Open Society—Georgia Foundation, online at http://www.ifsdeurope.com/presentation.html.

Udensiva-Brenner, M., 2010. "Kakha Bendukidze Analyzes Georgia's Economic Strategy: How Georgia Handled Its Economy After the War and the Economic Crisis." *At The Harriman Institute*, April 7, online at http://www.harrimaninstitute.org/MEDIA/01716.pdf.

UN (United Nations), and WB (World Bank), 2009. *Georgia Joint Needs Assessment. Donor Funding in Support of Post-Conflict Recovery and Reconstruction. Progress Report*, June 30. New York and Washingtonm D.C.: The United Nations and The World Bank, online at http://www.mof.ge/common/get_doc.aspx?doc_id=5994.

UNDP (United Nations Development Programme), 2010. "Indicators Human Development Index (HDI) – 2010 Rankings." *International Human Development.* UNDP, online at http://hdr.undp.org/en/statistics/.

Uzagalieva, A., 2007. "Economic Sanctions and Exports in Georgia." *Georgian Economic Trends*, April, online at http://www.geplac.ge/newfiles/GeorgianEconomicTrends/2007/englishapril2007.pdf.

Vaicenavičius, R. J., 2008. "Strengthening the Independence and Sustainable Functioning of the Department for Statistics in Georgia." *Georgian Economic Trends*, October, online at http://www.geplac.ge/newfiles/GeorgianEconomicTrends/2008/October%202008%20(eng).pdf.

Vincentz, V., 2006. "Diversifying and Promoting Exports in Georgia." *Georgian Economic Trends*, October, online at http://www.geplac.ge/files/english_october_2006.pdf.

Vincentz, V., 2008. "Trade Policy and Georgian Exports." *Georgian Economic Trends*, October, online at http://www.geplac.ge/newfiles/GeorgianEconomicTrends/2008/October%202008%20(eng).pdf.

Vreeland, J. R., 2003. *The IMF and Economic Development*. Cambridge: Cambridge University Press.

Walker, C., 2007. "The Rose Revolution, by the Numbers." *The National Interest*, December 13, online at http://nationalinterest.org/commentary/inside-track-the-rose-revolution-by-the-numbers-1906.

Wang, J.-Y., 1998. "From Coupon to Lari: Hyperinflation and Stabilization in Georgia." *Caucasica. The Journal of Caucasian Studies,* Vol. 1.

WB (World Bank), 2010. *Doing Business. Economy Rankings*. Washington, D.C.: The World Bank Group, online at http://www.doingbusiness.org/EconomyRankings/.

WB (World Bank), 2011. *The World Bank Group's Response to the Global Economic Crisis*. Washington, D.C.: The World Bank.

WEF (World Economic Forum), 2011. *Global Competitiveness Report 2010–2011*. Geneva: World Economic Forum, online at http://gcr.weforum.org/gcr2010/.

Wellisz, S., 1996. *Georgia: A Brief Survey of Macroeconomic Problems and Policies*. Studies and Analyses, Working Papers, No. 87. Warsaw: CASE.

Welt, C., 2004. "Georgia: Consolidating the Revolution." *CSIS Russia ans Eurasia Program.* 2004, April 6, online at http://csis.org/files/media/csis/pubs/ci.consolidatingrevolution.04.06.05.pdf.

Westley, C., 2008. "The Economics of War (Georgia Edition)." *Ludwig von Mises Institute Daily Article*, August 26, online at http://mises.org/story/3074.

Zevin, L., 2001. "The IMF and Russia: Eight Years of Difficult Dialogue." *Mirovaja ekonomika i mezdunarodnye otnosenija,* No. 4. (In Russian).

Zhvania, Z., 2004. "After the Rose Revolution: Building Georgia's Future." *CSIS Statesmen's Forum*. April 26, online at http://csis.org/files/media/csis/events/040426_zhvania_report.pdf.

ABOUT AUTHOR

Dr. Vladimer Papava is a Senior Fellow at the Georgian Foundation for Strategic and International Studies, a Chief Research Associate at the Paata Gugushvili Institute of Economics (Ivane Javakhishvili Tbilisi State University) and a Senior Associate Fellow of the Joint Transatlantic Research and Policy Center at the South Asia-Caucasus Institute (Johns Hopkins University-SAIS). He was the Minister of Economy of the Republic of Georgia (1994-2000) and a Member of Parliament (2004-2008) (Tbilisi, Republic of Georgia); in 2005-2006 he was a Fulbright Fellow at the Central Asia-Caucasus Institute, The Nitze School–SAIS, Johns Hopkins University (Washington, D.C.). He is the author more than 200 publications, including works on the theoretical and applied studies post-Communist economies and economic development of the Central Caucasus countries. Dr. Papava holds a Degree of the Candidate of Economic Sciences from Central Economic-Mathematical Institute of the Academy of Sciences of the USSR (1982, Moscow, Russia), a Degree of the Doctor of Economic Sciences from Leningrad State University (1990, Saint-Petersburg, Russia), and Tbilisi State University (1989, Tbilisi, Georgia). His English-language publications include: *Financial Globalization and Post-Communist Georgia* (New York: iUniverse, 2003) with Vepkhia Chocheli, *Splendours and Miseries of the IMF in Post-Communist Georgia* (Laredo, TX, 2003), *Necroeconomics: The Political Economy of Post-Communist Capitalism* (New York: iUniverse, 2005), *The Central Caucasus: Problems of Geopolitical Economy* (New York: Nova Science Publishers, 2008) with Eldar Ismailov, and *Rethinking Central Eurasia* (Washington, D.C.: Johns Hopkins University-SAIS, Stockholm: Institute for Security and Development Policy, 2010) also with Eldar Ismailov.

INDEX

A

B

C

D

E

F

G

H

I

O

P

R

U

V

W

Y

Z